NATIONAL STANDARDS
FOR CIVICS AND GOVERNMENT

Center for Civic Education

DIRECTED BY THE

Center for Civic Education

AND FUNDED BY THE

U. S. Department Education

AND THE

Pew Charitable Trusts

ISBN 0-89818-155-0

Contents

Preface

I know of no safe depository of the ultimate powers of the society but the people themselves; and if we think them not enlightened enough to exercise their control with a wholesome discretion, the remedy is not to take it from them, but to inform their discretion.

Thomas Jefferson (1820)

It has been recognized since the founding of the nation that education has a civic mission: to prepare informed, rational, humane, and participating citizens committed to the values and principles of American constitutional democracy. This civic mission of the schools has recently been reaffirmed in the National Education Goals included in the Goals 2000: Educate America Act of 1994.

Goal 3 Student Achievement and Citizenship

By the year 2000, all students will leave grades 4, 8, and 12 having demonstrated competency over challenging subject matter including...civics and government...so that they may be prepared for responsible citizenship, further learning, and productive employment....

All students will be involved in activities that promote and demonstrate...good citizenship, community service, and personal responsibility.

Goal 6 Adult Literacy and Lifelong Learning

By the year 2000, every adult American will be literate and will possess the knowledge and skills necessary to...exercise the rights and responsibilities of citizenship.

To help achieve these goals, the Center for Civic Education (Center) has developed these voluntary *National Standards for Civics and Government* for students in kindergarten through grade twelve (K-12) supported by the Office of Educational Research and Improvement (OERI) of the U.S. Department of Education and The Pew Charitable Trusts.

These *National Standards for Civics and Government* are intended to help schools develop competent and responsible citizens who possess a reasoned commitment to the fundamental values and principles that are essential to the preservation and improvement of American constitutional democracy.

This document is limited to **content standards** specifying what students should know and be able to do in the field of civics and government. Content standards are **not** course outlines. They are **"exit" standards**; they specify what students should know and be able to do as they "exit"or complete the 4th, 8th, and 12th grades. Achievement of these standards should be fostered not only by explicit attention to civic education in the curriculum, but also in related subjects such as history, literature, geography, economics, and the sciences and by the informal curriculum of the school, the pattern of relations maintained in the school and its governance. To achieve the standards students must be provided with the kinds of learning opportunities in the classroom, school, and community that foster the skills necessary for civic participation.

Standards alone cannot improve student achievement, teacher performance, or school quality, but they can be an important stimulus for change. They provide widely agreed upon guidelines for what all students in this nation should learn and be able to do in the field of civics and government. They are useful in the development of curricular frameworks, course outlines, textbooks, professional development programs, and systems of assessment. These national standards are voluntary. They are provided as a resource to state and local education agencies and others interested in the improvement of education in civics and government.

These standards should not be considered to be a static or "finished" document. They should form the basis for continuing discussion, and they will be revised periodically in light of research, new scholarship, and public commentary.

The Center wishes to express its appreciation to the many people who have contributed to the development of the *National Standards for Civics and Government*, and to the funding agencies that supported the project. The developmental process benefitted from the comments of persons who have participated in more than one hundred-fifty open hearings and public discussions of the standards. Well over one thousand teachers and other educators, scholars, parents, elected officials, and representatives of public and private organizations and groups have provided critical comments on successive drafts in the two-year developmental period. Leaders in civic education from numerous other nations also have shared the benefit of their experience and provided valuable insights in the standards-setting process. Names of all colleagues who have provided written critiques are listed in the appendices.

The Center has attempted to be responsive to the many excellent suggestions received. Our aim has been to provide a useful and balanced document reflecting a broad consensus among educators, scholars, and others who have contributed to the development of these standards. Any shortcomings in the standards are the responsibility of the Center.

Ultimately, the value of these standards will be determined in the classroom by knowledgeable, skilled, and dedicated teachers who have the capacity to make the study of civics and government the relevant, vital, and inspiring experience it should be. Teachers who foster students' natural, youthful idealism, and commitment to working together enhance the realization of the goals of American constitutional democracy.

Introduction

I. Rationale for education in civics and government

There is an old saying that the course of civilization is a race between catastrophe and education. In a democracy such as ours, we must make sure that education wins the race.

John F. Kennedy (1958)

A. **The civic mission of the schools.** Although it has been argued that the establishment of the proper institutions is sufficient to maintain a free society, Thomas Jefferson, James Madison, John Adams, and others recognized that even the most well-designed institutions are not sufficient. Ultimately, a free society must rely on the knowledge, skills, and virtue of its citizens and those they elect to public office. Civic education, therefore, is essential to the preservation and improvement of American constitutional democracy.

The goal of education in civics and government is informed, responsible participation in political life by competent citizens committed to the fundamental values and principles of American constitutional democracy. Their effective and responsible participation requires the acquisition of a body of knowledge and of intellectual and participatory skills. Effective and responsible participation also is furthered by development of certain dispositions or traits of character that enhance the individual's capacity to participate in the political process and contribute to the healthy functioning of the political system and improvement of society.

Many institutions help to develop Americans' knowledge and skills and shape their civic character and commitments. The family, religious institutions, the media, and community groups exert important influences. Schools, however, bear a special and historic responsibility for the development of civic competence and civic responsibility. Schools fulfill that responsibility through both formal and informal curricula beginning in the earliest grades and continuing through the entire educational process.

Formal instruction in civics and government should provide students with a basic understanding of civic life, politics, and government. It should help them understand the workings of their own and other political systems as well as the relationship of American politics and government to world affairs. Formal instruction provides a basis for understanding the rights and responsibilities of citizens in American constitutional democracy and a framework for competent and responsible participation. The formal curriculum should be augmented by related learning experiences, in both school and community, that enable students to learn how to participate in their own governance.

In addition to the formal curriculum, the importance of the informal curriculum should be recognized. The informal curriculum refers to the governance of the school community and relationships among those within it. These relationships should embody the fundamental values and principles of American constitutional democracy. Classrooms and schools should be managed by adults who govern in accordance with constitutional values and principles and who display traits of character worth emulating. Students should be held accountable for behaving in accordance with fair and reasonable standards and for respecting the rights and dignity of others, including their peers.

B. The need for increased attention to civic education. Although the National Education Goals, as well as the goals, curricular requirements, and policies of every state, express the need for and extol the value of civic education, this vital part of the student's overall education is seldom given sustained and systematic attention in the K-12 curriculum. Inattention to civic education stems in part from the assumption that the knowledge and skills citizens need emerge as by-products of the study of other disciplines or as an outcome of the process of schooling itself.

While it is true that history, economics, literature, and other subjects do enhance students' understanding of government and politics, they cannot replace sustained, systematic attention to civic education. Civics should be seen as a central concern from kindergarten through twelfth grade, whether it is taught as a part of other curricula or in separate units or courses.

Civics and government should be seen as a discipline equal to others. Civics and government, like history and geography, is an interdisciplinary subject, whose substance is drawn from the disciplines of political science, political philosophy, history, economics, and jurisprudence.

In sum, civic education should not be considered incidental to the schooling of American youth. Civic education instead should be considered central to the purposes of American education and essential to the well-being of American democracy. It is particularly important for students in less privileged socio-economic circumstances. Research tells us that if these students are to have the opportunity to acquire the knowledge and skills essential for informed, effective citizenship, it must be provided at elementary and secondary levels of their education.

"Government of the people, by the people, and for the people," in Lincoln's phrase, means that the people have the right to control their government. But this right is meaningless unless they have the knowledge and skills to exercise that control and possess the traits of character required to do so responsibly.

II. Goals and standards

The following definitions should be kept in mind while reading the standards document.

A. Goals. Goals are statements of the overarching aims or ends of education such as fostering the development of competent and responsible citizens.

B. Standards. In the continuing effort to improve education in the United States, standards of varying kinds have been identified.

- **Standards for students.** Standards for students are statements specifying what students should know and be able to do, as well as the level of achievement that is to be expected of them. Standards for students include **content standards** and **performance standards**.

- **Content standards.** Content standards are statements of what students should know and be able to do in a specific discipline such as civics, history, or geography. Content standards are concerned with the knowledge students should acquire and the understandings they should develop, as well as with the intellectual and participatory skills students should develop in the course of their K-12 experience.

  - **Performance standards.** Performance standards are criteria for determining students' levels of achievement of content standards.

- **Standards for teachers.** Standards for teachers are criteria for determining whether teachers have the capacity to assist their students in attaining high content and performance standards. These criteria include the adequacy of their preparation in the subjects they will teach, their ability to communicate their knowledge, their pedagogical skills, and the degree to which they stay abreast of their academic and professional disciplines.

- **Standards for schools.** Standards for schools are called delivery, equity or opportunity-to-learn standards. They are intended to guarantee insuring an equitable educational environment by insuring that all children have the opportunity to learn challenging subject matter.

- **Standards for state and local education agencies.** Standards for state and local education agencies are criteria for judging the success of state and local educational agencies.

III. Content standards and intellectual and participatory skills

The content standards in this document specify not only the content to be mastered in civics and government, but also what students should be able to do in relation to that content. These standards include, either explicitly or implicitly, a specification of the intellectual and participatory skills students should acquire.

A. **Intellectual skills.** Intellectual skills in civics and government are inseparable from content. To be able to think critically about a political issue, for example, one must have an understanding of the issue, its history, and its contemporary relevance, as well as a set of intellectual tools or considerations useful in dealing with such an issue.

Many of the content standards require that "Students should be able to evaluate, take, and defend positions about... " a particular topic or issue. These standards are followed by subsidiary statements which are intended to specify the knowledge and intellectual skills required to attain the standard.

For example, the following standard is from the grade 9-12 standards:

Part III, E. "How does the American political system provide for choice and opportunities for participation?" on page 118-119.

3. **Political communication: television, radio, the press, and political persuasion.** *Students should be able to evaluate, take, and defend positions on the influence of the media on American political life.*

   To achieve this standard, students should be able to

   - explain the meaning and importance of freedom of the press

   - evaluate the role in American politics of television, radio, the press, newsletters, data bases, and emerging means of communication, e.g., the internet, faxes, electronic mail

   - compare and contrast various forms of political persuasion and discuss the extent to which traditional forms have been replaced by electronic media

   - explain how Congress, the president, state and local public officials use the media to communicate with the citizenry

   - evaluate historical and contemporary political communications using such criteria as logical validity, factual accuracy, emotional appeal, distorted evidence, appeals to bias or prejudice, e.g.,

     - speeches such as Lincoln's "House Divided," Sojourner Truth's "Ain't I a Woman?", Chief Joseph's "I Shall Fight No More Forever," Roosevelt's "Four Freedoms," Martin Luther King Jr.'s "I Have a Dream"

     - government wartime information programs

     - campaign advertisements

     - political cartoons

B. **Terms used to identify intellectual skills.** Verbs in common usage are used in these content standards to identify the intellectual skills which students should develop. For example, the standards require students to "describe," "explain," "evaluate," and "take and defend" positions. These verbs were chosen rather than those found in some taxonomies used by professional curriculum developers because they are readily understandable by a broader audience—parents, students, and the larger community.

The use of these verbs should **not** be interpreted to mean that the standards do not call for the development of higher-order thinking skills. Descriptions, explanations, and the evaluation, adoption, and defense of positions can range from basic intellectual tasks to those of the highest order.

The following are the verbs most commonly used in the standards and the intellectual skills they specify. It should be noted that each verb, such as the verb "identify," may specify a skill that may be exercised at a range of levels, from the very simple act, for example, of identifying a member of Congress in a particular district, to identifying the criteria being used in a Supreme Court opinion.

1. **"Identify."** To identify things that are tangible (one's representative) or intangible (justice). To identify something may involve being able to (1) distinguish it from something else, (2) classify or catalog something with other items with similar attributes or, in some cases, (3) determine its origin.

2. **"Describe."** To describe tangible or intangible objects, processes, institutions, functions, purposes, means and ends, qualities. To describe something is to be able to give a verbal or written account of its basic attributes or characteristics.

3. **"Explain."** To identify, describe, clarify, or interpret something. One may explain (1) causes of events, (2) the meaning or significance of events or ideas, (3) reasons for various acts or positions.

4. **"Evaluate a position."** To use criteria or standards to make judgments about the (1) strengths and weaknesses of a position on a particular issue, (2) goals promoted by the position, or (3) means advocated to attain the goals.

5. **"Take a position."** To use criteria or standards to arrive at a position one can support (1) one may select from alternative positions, or (2) create a novel position.

6. **"Defend a position."** To (1) advance arguments in favor of one's position and (2) respond to or take into account arguments opposed to one's position

C. **Participatory skills.** Education in civics and government must not only address the acquisition of knowledge and intellectual skills; it also must focus specifically on the development of those skills required for competent participation in the political process. These include such skills as

   - the capacity to influence policies and decisions by working with others

   - clearly articulating interests and making them known to key decision and policy makers

   - building coalitions, negotiating, compromising, and seeking consensus

   - managing conflicts

Center for Civic Education

Participatory skills are developed by providing students with opportunities to practice these skills and to observe and interact with those in their community who are adept in exercising them.

Learning opportunities useful in fostering participatory skills include:

1. **Monitoring politics and government.** Students should learn how to monitor the handling of issues by the political process and by government. To help them attain this skill, they might be assigned to

   - track an issue in the media; research the issue in libraries; gather information from interest groups, members of government, and government agencies

   - perform research tasks in the community, such as interviewing people in public and private sectors involved in the political process, or observing meetings and hearings of public and private sector groups dealing with particular issues

   - report and reflect on their experiences

2. **Influencing politics and government.** Students should learn how to influence politics and government. To help them attain this skill, they can

   - take part in the politics and governance of their classrooms and schools by working in groups to reach agreements about school rules, assuming roles of authority, campaigning for student offices, advocating desired changes in school policy, and taking part in student courts

   - take part in simulations of the activities of government and private sector agencies and organizations, e.g., town meetings, administrative and legislative hearings, judicial hearings such as mock trials and moot courts, policy development meetings of organized groups, lobbying, nominating conventions, campaigns and elections, model UN meetings

   - observe governmental agencies and private sector organizations at work

   - learn how members of government and private organizations attempt to influence public policy by listening and talking to representatives visiting their classrooms

   - present positions to student councils, school administrators, school boards

   - write letters to newspapers and members of government

   - meet with members of government to advocate their positions

   - testify before public bodies

   - perform service in their schools or communities directly related to civic life, politics, and government

IV. Performance standards

Performance standards are statements of criteria to be used to measure levels of student achievement of content standards. These criteria may be used, for example, to assess a student's written or oral performance related to a specific content standard. An illustrative performance standard specifying three levels (basic, proficient, and advanced) of increasingly sophisticated student responses, each including and expanding on the previous level, is included in an appendix to this document. A complete set of performance standards to accompany these content standards will be developed by the Center if funding becomes available.

V. Vocabulary used in content standards

These standards are multidisciplinary; they draw most heavily from the fields of political philosophy, political science, constitutional law and jurisprudence, and history. Two criteria have guided the selection of vocabulary for the standards: (1) those terms most essential for all students and (2) those terms most useful in understanding the world of politics and government.

In the first instance, the standards have refrained from using some of the terms of scholarly discourse and, in some cases, have used commonly known synonyms when it appeared useful to do so. In the second instance, the standards employ terms required to understand the world of politics and government. The standards, therefore, have sometimes used terms from scholarly discourse that may not be generally familiar, because they are useful in describing and understanding politics and government.

Some essential terms not in common usage or which might be misunderstood are described briefly. These and other terms are defined in the standards or included in the glossary.

A. **Civic life/private life**. Civic life is the public life of the citizen concerned with the affairs of the community and nation, that is, the public realm. Private life, by comparison, is the personal life of the individual devoted to the pursuit of private interests.

B. **Civil society.** Civil society is the sphere of voluntary personal, social, and economic relationships and organizations that, although limited by law, is not part of governmental institutions. Civil society provides a domain where individuals are free from unreasonable interference from government. Many people argue that civil society, by providing for centers of political power outside government, is an indispensable means of maintaining limited government.

C. **Constitution.** The term "constitution" has various meanings, and constitutions serve differing purposes in different nations. In some nations a constitution is merely a description of a form of government. In the United States, as well as in some other nations, a constitution is a form of higher law that establishes and limits government in order to protect individual rights as well as to promote the common good. In the United States, constitutional government is equated with limited government.

Center for Civic Education

D. Liberalism. In addition to the experience of limited self-government during the colonial period and the experience of the American Revolution, the development of American constitutional democracy has been influenced by several intellectual traditions. Two of the most important of these are the complementary but sometimes contradictory philosophical traditions of **classical republicanism** and **liberalism**. Classical republicanism emphasizes the ideal of the common good while liberalism stresses individual rights. The Preamble of the United States Constitution contains ideals often associated with republicanism. The Declaration of Independence is a classic and succinct statement of the central ideas of liberal theory.

The term "liberal" is derived from "liberty." The ideas associated with liberalism were developed during the Protestant Reformation, the rise of market economies and free enterprise, and were further elaborated during the eighteenth-century Enlightenment. Liberalism refers to a political theory developed by thinkers such as John Locke. They argued that the principal purpose of government is the protection of individual rights, the "unalienable rights to life, liberty, and the pursuit of happiness," of which Jefferson spoke in the Declaration of Independence. They also held that the authority of the government is based on the consent of the people. That authority, they insisted, should be limited to the protection of individual rights.

A liberal democracy is a democracy based on the ideas of liberalism, the most important of which are the protection of individual rights and consent of the governed as the basis of political authority. Historians and political scientists have characterized most of the advanced western democracies as "liberal democracies." The United States is a classic example of this form of government. Since "liberal" is often used to identify a position on the liberal–conservative political spectrum in American politics, these standards classify the United States as a "constitutional democracy" rather than a "liberal democracy" and limit the treatment of the history of liberalism and liberal democracy to the standards at the 9-12 level.

E. Republicanism. Republics are states governed by elected representatives of the people. Republics can be contrasted to monarchies. While monarchs traditionally ruled by personal authority over their subjects, the government of republics is in principle the common concern of the people (*res publica*, "thing of the people"). Republics are similar to direct democracies in that sovereignty lies in the whole citizenry; but republics differ from direct democracies in that power is usually exercised by elected representatives rather than directly by the people.

The American Founders were influenced by the republican ideas of both ancient Greece and Rome. Classical republicanism, especially in Rome, stressed two central ideas. One was that the primary purpose of government is to promote the common good of the whole society rather than that of one particular class or segment of society. The second purpose was the necessity for the civic virtue of its citizens. Civic virtue requires the citizen to place the public or common good above private interest.

F. Politics. Politics is the process by which a group of people, whose opinions or interests might be divergent (1) reach collective decisions that are generally regarded as binding on the group and enforced as common policy, (2) seek the power to influence decisions about such matters as how their government will manage the distribution of resources, the allocation of benefits and burdens, and the management of conflicts, and (3) accomplish goals they could not realize as individuals.

G. Systems of shared powers. Although the political system of the United States has traditionally been called a presidential system or system of separated powers, these terms do not reflect the reality of the complex system of dispersed powers created by the Constitution. It is inaccurate to say, for example, that the power to make laws has been separated and given solely to the legislature.

Although powers are separated among the different branches of national, state, and local governments, they also are shared. Each branch shares some of the powers and functions of the other branches. For example, although Congress may pass laws, the president may veto them. Some law, administrative law, is created by the executive branch. Finally, Congress passes laws, but the Supreme Court may review their constitutionality.

Contemporary students of government increasingly refer to the United States and nations with similar arrangements for the distribution, sharing, and limitation of powers as "systems of shared powers," because this phrase is a more accurate description than the term "separation of powers." It is therefore being used in these standards.

H. Citizens and Americans. The term "citizen" is used throughout this document in a broad, encompassing sense. For example, students are citizens of their classroom and their school. They also are citizens of their neighborhood and community. As a matter of fact, many of the rights, responsibilities, and citizenship activities described in these standards apply to all residents of the United States and its territories, not to natural-born or naturalized citizens alone. Section V.1.A., of the 5-8 and 9-12 standards, however, does define citizenship more precisely where it is appropriate to do so.

The term "Americans" also is used throughout this document. While it is true that others in the Western Hemisphere also consider themselves to be "Americans," that name generally is recognized as designating the people of the United States of America.

VI. Audiences and uses of national standards

The principal audiences for this document are

A. Teachers. Content standards provide teachers with clear statements of what they should teach their students. They promote fairness by providing teachers with adequate notice of what is expected of them.

B. **Teacher education and credentialing institutions.**
Standards provide teacher education and credentialing
institutions with clear guidelines for training teachers and
granting credentials. Specifying what students from kindergarten
through grade twelve should know and be able to do will give
guidance for pre-service course selection and help ensure that
teachers themselves benefit from a rigorous curriculum.

C. **Assessment specialists.** Standards are essential to the
development of assessment programs designed to determine
acceptable levels of performance.

D. **Parents and the community.** Standards will provide parents
and other community members with understandable information
about what should be taught and learned in K-12 education.

E. **Curriculum developers.** Standards provide guidance for the
development of high quality curricular programs, textbooks, and
other related educational materials.

F. **Policy makers.** Standards and evidence of their achievement
provide a rational basis for the development and implementation
of public policy in education.

K-4 Content Standards

K-4 Content Standards

I. WHAT IS GOVERNMENT AND WHAT SHOULD IT DO?

A. What is government?

Content summary and rationale

At the early elementary level, **government** can be described as the people and groups within a society with the authority to make, carry out, and enforce laws and to manage disputes about them. Understanding what government does may be initiated in early grades by having students look at the governance of the family and school as analogous to the governance of the larger community and the nation. In the family, for example, parents make rules governing the behavior of their children. They also are responsible for enforcing these rules and for settling disputes when conflicts arise about them. In schools, teachers and administrators make, carry out, and enforce rules and laws and manage disputes about them.

These fundamental ideas about government and its functions provide a basis on which children in their earliest school years can begin to develop an understanding of the formal and informal institutions and processes of government in their communities, states, and the nation.

Content standards

1. **Defining government.** *Students should be able to provide a basic description of government.*

   To achieve this standard, students should be able to

   ■ describe government in terms of the people and groups who make, apply, and enforce rules and laws for others in their family, school, community, and nation and who manage disputes about them, e.g.,

     ■ adult family members make, apply, and enforce rules for their children and manage disputes about them

     ■ teachers, principals, and school boards make, apply, and enforce rules and laws for their schools and manage disputes about them

     ■ city councils and mayors make, apply, and enforce rules and laws for their communities

     ■ governors and state legislatures make, apply, and enforce rules and laws for their states

     ■ tribal governments make, apply, enforce rules and laws for tribal members in Indian country

     ■ the national government makes, applies, and enforces rules and laws for the nation

     ■ courts at all levels apply laws, manage disputes, and punish lawbreakers

Government can be described as the people and groups within a society with the authority to make, carry out, and enforce laws and to manage disputes about them.

B. Where do people in government get the authority to make, apply, and enforce rules and laws and manage disputes about them?

Content summary and rationale

Since government is defined as people and groups with **authority** to perform certain functions in a society, it is important to understand the concept of **authority** and the related concept of **power**. **Power** may be understood, in its relationship to government, as the capacity to direct or control someone or something. As such, power is a neutral term, it may be directed to good or bad ends. **Authority** is power that people have the right to use because of custom, law, or consent of the governed. In the United States, the authority of the government comes from the consent of the people.

Authority may be understood, at the elementary level, as the right of people in certain positions, such as parent, guardian, teacher, police officer, or president, to direct or control others. In the case of parents, authority comes from law and custom. People in other positions of authority gain the right to direct or control others by being appointed or elected. Students at an early age can understand that the person employed as a teacher has the right to teach the class and control the behavior of the students in it. A crossing guard has the right to control traffic and pedestrians. That right comes from laws that establish the position and describe the duties persons taking the position must fulfill. Those laws were made by others in positions of authority, such as legislators, selected by the people to represent them.

An understanding of the difference between power and authority is essential for understanding whether people with power have the right to exercise it.

Governments are instituted among Men, deriving their just Powers from the Consent of the Governed....
Declaration of Independence (1776)

Content standards

1. **Defining power and authority.** *Students should be able to explain the difference between authority and power without authority, and that authority comes from custom, law, and the consent of the governed.*

    To achieve this standard, students should be able to

    - explain that **power** is the ability to direct or control something or someone

    - explain that **authority** is power that people have the right to use because of custom, law, or the consent of the governed

        - parents have authority to direct and control their children; this authority comes from both custom and law

        - governors of states have the authority to carry out and enforce laws; this authority comes from law and the consent of the people who have elected the governors

    - identify examples of authority, e.g., the authority of teachers and administrators to make rules for schools, the authority of a crossing guard to direct traffic, the authority of the president to command the armed forces

    - identify examples of power without authority, e.g., a neighborhood bully forcing younger children to give up their lunch money, a robber holding up a bank

C. Why is government necessary?

Content summary and rationale

Many people have argued that life without government would be dangerous and miserable. Unfortunately, evidence supporting this claim is provided daily by events in some communities in the United States and in other nations where the controlling influences of government are weak or non-existent. It also is clear that government, when directed toward worthy purposes and conducted effectively in accord with basic principles of justice, can be a powerful force for the protection of the rights of individuals and the promotion of the common good.

An understanding of the necessity of government and its usefulness in promoting agreed upon goals which benefit the individual and society is essential for the development of informed, competent and responsible citizens.

Life without government would be dangerous and miserable.

Content standards

1. **Necessity and purposes of government.** *Students should be able to explain why government is necessary in their classroom, school, community, state, and nation, and the basic purposes of government in the United States.*

   To achieve this standard, students should be able to

   ■ explain probable consequences of the absence of government and of rules and laws

     ■ the strong may take advantage of the weak and act in their own selfish interests

     ■ people may become disorderly or violent and threaten others' lives, liberty, and property

     ■ people would feel insecure, unable to plan for the future, or to predict how others would behave, e.g., if there were no traffic laws, people could not predict on which side of the road cars would drive or that drivers would stop at red lights

   ■ explain that the basic purposes of government in the United States are to protect the rights of individuals and to promote the common good

D. What are some of the most important things governments do?

Governments make, carry out, enforce, and manage conflicts over rules and laws.

Content summary and rationale

An understanding of the basic things governments do may be developed by an examination of how schools and local communities make, carry out, enforce, and manage conflicts over rules and laws.

Understanding at the school and community level provides a basis for understanding how similar functions of government are carried out at state and national levels. It also may help students develop a more positive attitude toward government and an interest in participating in its activities.

Laws can protect rights, provide benefits, and assign responsibilities.

1. **Functions of government.** *Students should be able to explain some of the major things governments do in their school, community, state, and nation.*

   To achieve this standard, students should be able to

   ■ describe some major things governments do

   - **make laws** that establish schools, provide health services, and require licenses for drivers
   - **carry out laws** that provide for crossing guards at schools, build and maintain highways, conduct immunization programs
   - **enforce laws** that require people to obey traffic, health, child labor, and sanitation laws
   - **manage conflicts** so that disputes between people can be settled peacefully
   - **provide for the defense of the nation**

   ■ explain how government makes it possible for people working together to accomplish goals they could not achieve alone

E. What are the purposes of rules and laws?

In families and in less complex societies, customs, traditions, and rules play an important role in guiding behavior and establishing order. In more complex societies, laws are enacted to perform similar functions.

Laws can be used to provide order, predictability, and security.

Laws can be used to provide order, predictability, and security. Laws describe ways people should behave, and they can protect rights, provide benefits, and assign responsibilities.

A constitutional democracy such as the United States is governed by a rule of law that applies not only to the governed, but also to those who govern.

Law, its uses, and its influence are pervasive in the United States. An understanding of how it is used and its potential for promoting agreed upon ends is essential to an understanding of government.

Law, strictly understood, has as its first and principal object the ordering of the common good.

St. Thomas Aquinas (13th Century)

1. **Purposes of rules and laws.** *Students should be able to explain the purposes of rules and laws and why they are important in their classroom, school, community, state, and nation.*

   To achieve this standard, students should be able to

   ■ explain that rules and laws can be used to

   - **describe ways people should behave,** e.g., attend school and do homework, raise one's hand and be recognized before speaking in class, respect other peoples' privacy and property
   - **provide order, predictability, and security,** e.g., rules that require people to take turns, traffic laws that require people to drive on the right side of the street, laws that protect people from others who want to harm them or take their property

Center for Civic Education

- **protect rights**, e.g., laws that protect people's right to practice whatever religion they wish to, laws that provide equal opportunities for all students to get a free, public education

- **provide benefits**, e.g., laws that provide for schools, health services, public transportation, highways and airports

- **assign burdens or responsibilities**, e.g., laws that require people to pay taxes or to perform military service in times of national emergency

- **limit the power of people in authority**, e.g., laws that require teachers and school administrators to treat all students fairly, laws that prevent parents from abusing their children

F. How can you evaluate rules and laws?

Content summary and rationale

Not every rule or law is a good one. It is important, therefore, that young children become familiar with criteria that can be used to identify the strengths and weaknesses of rules or laws. It also is important that they learn to draft rules or laws that meet that criteria. An understanding of criteria useful in evaluating rules and laws also is important for adult Americans. It provides citizens with a basis for participating intelligently in the evaluation of existing and proposed laws.

Not every rule or law is a good one.

Content standards

1. **Evaluating rules and laws**. *Students should be able to explain and apply criteria useful in evaluating rules and laws.*

   To achieve this standard, students should be able to

   - identify the strengths and weaknesses of a school rule or a state law by determining if it is
     - well designed to achieve its purposes
     - understandable, i.e., clearly written; purposes are explicit
     - possible to follow, i.e., does not demand the impossible
     - fair, i.e., not biased against or for any individual or group
     - designed to protect individual rights and promote the common good
   - draft a school rule that meets these criteria

G. What are the differences between limited and unlimited governments?

Limits on government are designed to protect fundamental values and principles and to insure that government serves the purposes for which it was established.

Content summary and rationale

A limited government is one in which everyone, including all of the people in positions of authority, must obey the laws. In the United States, effective limitations are placed upon those in authority by the Constitution and Bill of Rights and numerous other laws. These limits are designed to protect fundamental values and principles and to insure that government serves the purposes for which it was established. Unlimited governments, by contrast, are those in which there are no effective controls over those in power.

An understanding of the differences between limited and unlimited government provides a basis for making reasoned judgments about whether people in authority are acting in accord with the responsibilities they have been assigned and the limitations placed upon their powers.

Content standards

1. **Limited and unlimited governments.** *Students should be able to explain the basic differences between limited and unlimited governments.*

    To achieve this standard, students should be able to

    ■ explain that in a limited government everyone, including all the people in positions of authority, must obey the laws. This even includes the president of the United States

    ■ give examples of laws that limit the power of people in government, e.g.,

      ■ laws that prohibit a teacher from releasing personal information about students to people other than their parents or guardians

      ■ laws that prohibit governments from discriminating against people because of their religious or political beliefs

    ■ explain that an unlimited government is one in which there are no effective controls over the powers of its rulers, who cannot be easily removed from office by peaceful, legal means, e.g., governments run by dictators

H. Why is it important to limit the power of government?

Content summary and rationale

In the United States, the powers of government are limited to insure that people in positions of authority fulfill the responsibilities they have been assigned, serve the major purposes of government, and do not misuse or abuse the power they have been given. Limited government thus is seen as essential to the protection of the rights of individuals.

An understanding of the reasons for and the necessity of limited government is essential if citizens are to control their government and make sure it fulfills its purposes.

Content standards

1. **Importance of limited government.** *Students should be able to explain why limiting the powers of government is important to their own lives.*

To achieve this standard, students should be able to

- explain why limited government is important for the protection of individual rights such as

    - **personal rights** to

        - choose their own friends

        - believe what they wish

        - enjoy the privacy of their homes

        - practice the religion of their choice

    - **political rights** to

        - express their opinions

        - vote

        - meet or associate with others

        - ask government to change laws they think are unfair

    - **economic rights** to

        - choose the kind of work they please

        - own property

Center for Civic Education

II. WHAT ARE THE BASIC VALUES AND PRINCIPLES OF AMERICAN DEMOCRACY?

A. What are the most important values and principles of American democracy?

Content summary and rationale

The fundamental values and principles of American democracy provide common ground for Americans to work together to promote the attainment of individual, community, and national goals.

These values and principles are expressed in the Declaration of Independence, the Constitution, the Gettysburg Address, and other significant documents, speeches, and writings.

Students' understanding of these fundamental values and principles and their importance for themselves, their community, and their nation is an essential first step in fostering a reasoned commitment to them. This commitment is essential to the preservation and improvement of American democracy.

Content standards

1. **Fundamental values and principles.** *Students should be able to explain the importance of the fundamental values and principles of American democracy.*

   To achieve this standard, students should be able to

   - explain the importance for themselves, their school, their community, and their nation of each of the following fundamental **values** of American democracy:
     - individual rights to life, liberty, property, and the pursuit of happiness
     - the public or common good
     - justice
     - equality of opportunity
     - diversity
     - truth
     - patriotism

   - explain the importance for themselves, their school, their community, and their nation of each of the following fundamental **principles** of American democracy:
     - the people are sovereign; they are the ultimate source of the authority of the government—"We the People..." have created the government, given it limited power to protect their rights and promote the common good, and can remove people from office and change the government
     - the power of government is limited by law
     - people exercise their authority directly by voting for or against certain rules, laws, or candidates as well as by voting in community or town meetings

- people exercise their authority indirectly through representatives they elect to make, apply, and enforce laws and to manage disputes about them

- decisions are based on majority rule, but minority rights are protected

■ identify fundamental values and principles as they are expressed in the Declaration of Independence, Preamble to the United States Constitution, the Bill of Rights, Pledge of Allegiance, speeches, songs, and stories

B. What are some important beliefs Americans have about themselves and their government?

Content summary and rationale

Although the United States is one of the most diverse nations in the world, amidst this diversity there are a number of important values, principles, and beliefs that Americans hold in common. First among them is a commitment to the fundamental values and principles of American democracy, such as the right to freedom of religion, speech, the press, and to the rule of law. Americans also hold other beliefs and values in common such as the importance placed on the individual and individual rights, equality of opportunity, education, the law, work, and voluntarism.

An understanding of this unifying framework of commonly held values, principles, and beliefs provides a basis and common ground for understanding and working with others.

First among the ideas Americans hold in common is a commitment to the values and principles of American democracy, such as the right to freedom of religion, speech, and the press.

Content standards

1. **Distinctive characteristics of American society.** *Students should be able to identify some important beliefs commonly held by Americans about themselves and their government.*

    To achieve this standard, students should be able to describe the following beliefs commonly held by Americans

    ■ **Importance of the individual.** Students should be able to explain that Americans believe

    - a primary purpose of government is to protect the rights of the individual to life, liberty, property, and the pursuit of happiness

    - another important purpose of government is to promote the common good

    - individuals have the right to differ about politics, religion, or any other matter

    - individuals have the right to express their views without fear of being punished by their peers or their government

    - the vote of one individual should count as much as another's

    ■ **Importance of their school, community, state, and nation.** Students should be able to explain that Americans believe that

    - everyone should be concerned about the well-being of his/her school, community, state, and nation

An understanding of this unifying framework of commonly held values, principles, and beliefs provides a basis and common ground for understanding and working with others.

Equal rights for all, special privileges for none.

Thomas Jefferson (c.1780)

No one can make you feel inferior without your consent.

Eleanor Roosevelt (1937)

Education is essential for informed and effective citizenship.

I am not ashamed to confess that twenty-five years ago I was a hired laborer, hauling rails, at work on a flatboat— just what might happen to any poor man's son. I want every man to have [a] chance....

Abraham Lincoln (1860)

- people should try to improve the quality of life in their schools, communities, states, and nation
- people should help others who are less fortunate than they and assist them in times of need, emergency, or natural disaster

■ **Importance of equality of opportunity and equal protection of the law.** Students should be able to explain that Americans believe that

- all people have a right to equal opportunity in education, employment, housing, and to equal access to public facilities such as parks and playgrounds
- all people have a right to participate in political life by expressing their opinions and trying to persuade others; all citizens over 18 years of age have the right to vote; and citizens who meet age and other qualifications have the right to seek public office
- everyone has the right to be treated equally in the eyes of the law

■ **Importance of respect for the law.** Students should be able to explain that Americans believe that

- everyone, including government officials, must obey the law
- people have the right to work together to see that laws they consider unfair or unwise are changed by peaceful means

■ **Importance of education.** Students should be able to explain that Americans believe that

- education is essential for informed and effective citizenship
- education is important for earning a living
- everyone should take advantage of the opportunity to be educated
- everyone has a right to public education
- people with special needs should be provided with appropriate educational opportunities, e.g., students with disabilities, children of migrant workers, adults who need training for employment

■ **Importance of work.** Students should be able to explain that Americans believe that

- work is important to a person's independence and self-esteem
- work is important to the well-being of the family, community, state, and nation
- adults should work to support themselves and their dependents, unless they are ill
- all honest work is worthy of respect

■ **Importance of voluntarism.** Students should be able to explain that Americans believe that

- people should volunteer to help others in their family, schools, communities, state, nation, and the world
- volunteering is a source of individual satisfaction and fulfillment

C. Why is it important for Americans to share certain values, principles, and beliefs?

Content summary and rationale

In contrast to most other nations, the identity of an American is defined by shared political values, principles, and beliefs rather than by ethnicity, race, religion, class, language, gender, or national origin. These shared values and principles have helped to promote cohesion in the daily life of Americans and in times of crisis they have enabled Americans to find common ground with those who differ from them.

To understand their nation, citizens should appreciate the nature and importance of shared values, principles, and beliefs which provide a foundation for the stability of their government.

Content standards

1. **American identity**. *Students should be able to explain the importance of Americans sharing and supporting certain values, principles, and beliefs.*

   To achieve this standard, students should be able to

   - explain that Americans are united by the values, principles, and beliefs they share rather than by ethnicity, race, religion, class, language, gender, or national origin

   - explain the importance of shared values, principles, and beliefs to the continuation and improvement of American democracy

   - identify basic documents that set forth shared values, principles, and beliefs, e.g., Declaration of Independence, United States Constitution and Bill of Rights, Pledge of Allegiance

   - identify symbols used to depict Americans' shared values, principles, and beliefs and explain their meaning, e.g., the flag, Statue of Liberty, Statue of Justice, Uncle Sam, Great Seal, national anthem, oaths of office, and mottoes such as *E Pluribus Unum*

   - describe holidays Americans celebrate and explain how they reflect their shared values, principles, and beliefs, e.g., the Fourth of July, Labor Day, Memorial Day, Presidents' Day, Columbus Day, Thanksgiving, Veterans Day, Martin Luther King, Jr.'s Birthday

D. What are the benefits of diversity in the United States?

Content summary and rationale

Diversity has contributed to the vitality and creativity of the United States by increasing the range of viewpoints, ideas, customs, and choices available to each individual in almost every aspect of life.

An understanding of the benefits of diversity to the individual and society as well as some of its costs may reduce irrational conflicts and unfair discrimination and provide a basis for the equitable handling of conflicts that do arise.

The principle on which this country was founded and by which it has always been governed is that Americanism is a matter of the mind and heart; Americanism is not, and never was, a matter of race and ancestry. A good American is one who is loyal to this country and to our creed of liberty and democracy.
Franklin Delano Roosevelt (1943)

America is woven of many strands; I would recognize them and let it so remain…. Our fate is to become one and yet many.
Ralph Ellison (1952)

Content standards

1. **Diversity in American society.** *Students should be able to describe diversity in the United States and identify its benefits.*

   To achieve this standard, students should be able to

   - explain the meaning of the word diversity
   - identify common forms of diversity in the United States, e.g., ethnic, racial, religious, class, linguistic, gender, national origin
   - explain why there is so much diversity in the United States
   - describe some benefits of diversity, e.g., it
     - fosters a variety of viewpoints, new ideas, and fresh ways of looking at and solving problems
     - provides people with choices in the arts, music, literature, and sports
     - helps people appreciate cultural traditions and practices other than their own
   - describe some of the costs of diversity
     - people sometimes discriminate unfairly against others on the basis of their age, religious beliefs, race, or disability
     - members of different groups misunderstand each other and conflicts may arise

E. How should conflicts about diversity be prevented or managed?

Content summary and rationale

Conflicts arising from diversity are inevitable. Some conflicts however, can be prevented by enhancing communication, by learning how and why people differ and by sharing common beliefs and goals.

The fair management of conflicts that do arise can be achieved by adhering to fundamental principles of procedural justice such as providing an opportunity for all sides to present their points of view and by arranging for arbitration by an impartial third party.

Content standards

1. **Prevention and management of conflicts.** *Students should be able to identify and evaluate ways conflicts about diversity can be prevented and managed.*

   To achieve this standard, students should be able to

   - identify examples of conflicts caused by diversity, e.g., unfair discrimination on the basis of race, ethnicity, religion, language, and gender; alienation of one group from another; efforts to impose beliefs and customs on others
   - evaluate ways conflicts about diversity can be prevented, such as by
     - encouraging communication among different groups
     - identifying common beliefs, interests, and goals

- working together on school and community problems and projects
- learning about others' customs, beliefs, history, problems, hopes and dreams
- listening to different points of view
- focusing on the beliefs Americans share
- adhering to the values and principles of American democracy

- evaluate ways conflicts about diversity can be managed fairly, such as those which

  - provide opportunities for people to present their points of view, e.g., to the student council, school board, city council, court of law
  - arrange for an impartial individual or group to listen to all sides of a conflict and suggest solutions to problems

F. How can people work together to promote the values and principles of American democracy?

Content summary and rationale

A general agreement on the values and principles of American democracy provides a basis for people to come together to manage their differences and to promote the ideals upon which the nation is founded—the protection of the rights of the individual and the promotion of the common good. Students must learn that in order to protect their own rights, they must be responsible for supporting the rights of others, even those with whom they may disagree or dislike. To provide a safe and healthy community, all must agree to work together. This may mean merely refraining from littering or writing graffiti or it may mean volunteering for school or community service. It may also mean working with others to get new laws passed that will benefit themselves and their community.

I have a dream that my four little children will one day live in a nation where they will not be judged by the color of their skin but by the content of their character.
Martin Luther King, Jr.
(1963)

Content standards

1. **Promoting ideals.** *Students should be able to identify ways people can work together to promote the values and principles of American democracy.*

To achieve this standard, students should be able to

- explain how they can promote the values and principles of American democracy by

  - respecting the rights of others, e.g., allowing those with whom they disagree to express their views; not invading the privacy of others; not discriminating unfairly against others because of their race, ethnicity, language, gender, or religious beliefs
  - helping to promote the common good, e.g., volunteering for school and community service, cleaning up the environment
  - participating in government, e.g., voting, becoming informed about public issues, attempting to change laws by writing to legislators, serving on juries

III. HOW DOES THE GOVERNMENT ESTABLISHED BY THE CONSTITUTION EMBODY THE PURPOSES, VALUES, AND PRINCIPLES OF AMERICAN DEMOCRACY?

It should be made clear to all Americans at an early age that government is their servant, not their master.

A. What is the United States Constitution and why is it important?

Content summary and rationale

The United States Constitution is a written set of laws that

- states that the basic purposes of government are protecting the rights of individuals and promoting the common good

- organizes the government and grants and divides its powers among the legislative, executive, and judicial branches

- limits the powers of government to prevent their misuse or abuse

- makes it clear that the government is the servant of the people—the people created the government, they control it, and they have the right to change it and to remove anyone working in government who is failing to fulfill his or her responsibilities

Americans should learn at an early age that government is their servant, not their master. It exists to protect their rights and to promote the common good. The Constitution of the United States sets forth these purposes and it provides a basis for understanding the fundamental ideas underlying government and evaluating its actions.

Content standards

1. **The meaning and importance of the United States Constitution.** *Students should be able to describe what the United States Constitution is and why it is important.*

   To achieve this standard, students should be able to explain that the United States Constitution

   - is a written document that

     - states that the basic purposes of their government are to protect individual rights and promote the common good

     - describes how the government is organized

   - limits the powers of government by saying what government can and cannot do

   - is the highest law in the land; no government can make laws that take away rights it guarantees

   - was created by people who believed that the

     - government is established by and for the people

     - government is the servant of the people

     - the people have the right to choose their representatives

     - the people have the right to change their government and the United States Constitution

We the People of the United States...do ordain and establish this Constitution for the United States of America.
Preamble to the U.S. Constitution (1787)

B. What does the national government do and how does it protect individual rights and promote the common good?

Content summary and rationale

The national government established by the Constitution is responsible for making, carrying out, and enforcing laws, and managing conflicts over their interpretation and application. The national government is responsible for making laws that serve the purposes for which it was established—the protection of individual rights and promotion of the common good. The national government also is responsible for carrying out and enforcing laws and for seeing that disputes about laws are settled in a fair manner.

Children need to be introduced to the national government and the roles and responsibilities of its three branches. This introduction provides an initial basis for understanding the national government and how it goes about fulfilling its responsibilities. That understanding, when it is extended and deepened, enables citizens to evaluate the actions of the government and therefore to participate in it more effectively.

Government is responsible for making laws that serve the purposes for which it was established—the protection of individual rights and promotion of the common good.

Content standards

1. **Organization and major responsibilities of the national government**. *Students should be able to give examples of ways the national government protects individual rights and promotes the common good.*

   To achieve this standard, students should be able to explain that

   ■ Congress passes laws to

   - protect individual rights, e.g., laws protecting freedom of religion and expression and preventing unfair discrimination

   - promote the common good, e.g., laws providing for clean air, national parks, and the defense of the nation

   ■ the executive branch carries out and enforces laws to

   - protect individual rights, e.g., voting rights, equal opportunities to an education

   - promote the common good, e.g., enforcement of pure food and drug laws, enforcement of clean air laws

   ■ the judicial branch, headed by the Supreme Court, makes decisions concerning the law that are intended to

   - protect individual rights, e.g., the right to a fair trial, to vote, to practice one's religious beliefs

   - promote the common good, e.g., upholding laws that protect the rights of all people to equal opportunity

C. What are the major responsibilities of state governments?

Content summary and rationale

State governments are established by state constitutions, which have purposes and functions similar to the United States Constitution. Each state has its own legislative, executive, and judicial branch. State governments, along with their local and intermediate (county, parish, special districts) governments, affect every aspect of a citizen's life. The services of state and local governments are more familiar to younger students than are those of the national government. State governments create and carry out laws providing for public education, health care, parks, roads, and highways.

Understanding the major responsibilities and organization of state government provides the citizen with the knowledge required to request government services, judge how well government is fulfilling its responsibilities, and hold officials accountable for fulfilling their responsibilities.

Content standards

State governments, along with local governments affect many aspects of citizen's lives.

1. **Organization and major responsibilities of state governments.** *Students should be able to explain the most important responsibilities of their state government.*

   To achieve this standard, students should be able to

   - distinguish between the national and state governments

   - describe the major responsibilities of each branch of their state government

     - legislative branch—makes state laws, decides how the state will spend tax money, approves appointments made by the governor

     - executive branch—carries out and enforces laws made by the state legislature, e.g., laws providing for education, health care for needy children, protection of fish and game

     - judicial branch—interprets law and manages conflicts about the law

   - describe important services their state government provides, e.g., education, law enforcement, health services and hospitals, roads and highways, public welfare

   - describe how state government officials are chosen, e.g., elections, appointment

   - explain how people can participate in their state government, e.g., being informed and taking part in discussions of state issues, voting, volunteering their services, holding public office, serving on governing committees and commissions

   - explain why it is important that people participate in their state government, e.g., to protect their rights and promote the common welfare, improve the quality of life in their community, to gain personal satisfaction, to prevent officials from abusing their power

   - explain how state government services are paid for, e.g., taxes on sales and on individual and business income, fees for using parks and toll roads, license fees

Center for Civic Education

D. What are the major responsibilities of local governments?

Content summary and rationale

Local governments provide most of the services citizens receive, and local courts handle most civil disputes and violations of the law. State and local governments license businesses, professions, automobiles, and drivers; provide essential services such as police and fire protection, education, and street maintenance; regulate zoning and the construction of buildings; provide public housing, transportation, and public health services; and maintain streets, highways, airports, and harbors.

Local governments generally are more accessible to the people than their state and national governments. Members of city councils, boards of education, mayors, and other officials often are available to meet with individuals and groups and to speak to students and civic organizations. Meetings of local agencies are usually open to the public.

Citizens need to know the purposes, organization, and responsibilities of their local governments so they can take part in their governance.

Content standards

1. **Organization and major responsibilities of local governments.**
   Students should be able to explain the most important responsibilities of their local government.

   To achieve this standard, students should be able to

   - distinguish among national, state, and local governments
   - describe services commonly and primarily provided by local governments
     - public safety, e.g., police, fire, street lighting services
     - public utilities, e.g., water, gas, electricity
     - transportation, e.g., streets, highways, bus or subway systems, airports, harbors
     - education and recreation, e.g., schools, libraries, museums, parks, sports facilities
   - explain how local government services are paid for, e.g., property, sales, and other taxes; money from state and national governments
   - describe how local government officials are chosen, e.g., election, appointment
   - explain how people can participate in their local government, e.g., being informed and taking part in discussions of local issues, voting, volunteering their services, holding public office, serving on governing committees and commissions
   - explain why it is important that people participate in their local government, e.g., to protect their rights and promote the common good, improve the quality of life in their community, to gain personal satisfaction, to prevent officials from abusing their power

Local governments provide most of the services citizens receive, and local courts handle most civil disputes and violations of the law.

E. Who represents you in the legislative and executive branches of your local, state, and national governments?

Content summary and rationale

Few Americans can identify most of the key people elected to serve them. It is important to know not only who these people are but also what their positions are on important issues. It also is important to know what their responsibilities are, how well they are fulfilling them, and how they can be contacted on matters of interest. Such knowledge is essential for effective participation.

Content standards

1. **Identifying members of government.** *Students should be able to identify the members of the legislative branches and the heads of the executive branches of their local, state, and national governments.*

   To achieve this standard, students should be able to

   - name the persons representing them at state and national levels in the legislative branches of government, e.g., representatives and senators in their state legislature and in Congress

   - name the persons representing them at the executive branches of government, e.g., mayor, governor, president

   - explain how they can contact their representatives

   - explain which level of government they should contact to express their opinions or to get help on specific problems, e.g.,

     - crime
     - the environment
     - recreational opportunities in schools and parks
     - street lights
     - trash in the streets or vacant lots
     - stray or wild animals
     - abandoned cars
     - missing persons

Americans should know how to contact public officials.

IV. WHAT IS THE RELATIONSHIP OF THE UNITED STATES TO OTHER NATIONS AND TO WORLD AFFAIRS?

A. How is the world divided into nations?

Content summary and rationale

As a basis for understanding the place of the United States in the world, students must know that the world is divided into many different nations, each having its own government. Each nation is made up of its territory, people, laws, and government. The United States is one nation and it interacts with other nations.

Content standards

1. **Nations.** *Students should be able to explain that the world is divided into different nations which interact with one another.*

   To achieve this standard, students should be able to explain that

   - the world is divided into many different nations and that each has its own government

   - a nation consists of its territory, people, laws, and government

   - the United States is one nation and that it interacts with all other nations in the world

B. How do nations interact with one another?

Content summary and rationale

Nations interact by sending representatives to meet together to discuss common interests and problems. They often make treaties or agreements about such problems as the environment, drug trade, or mutual defense. Nations also interact by trading—buying and selling manufactured and agricultural goods such as farm equipment, food, television sets, and airplanes.

There is no international organization with power comparable to that of a sovereign nation. When conflicts arise, governmental representatives attempt to help nations manage their affairs and conflicts peacefully, but sometimes these conflicts result in the use of military force.

Resolving conflicts among nations peacefully through discussions and agreements promotes the rights of all people to life, liberty, and property and helps to promote the common good.

The United Nations (U.N.) is an international organization that provides a way for representatives of different nations to meet together to discuss their common interests and to attempt to solve problems peacefully. Sometimes the U.N. does this by sending peacekeeping forces to areas where there are conflicts.

Resolving conflicts among nations peacefully through discussions and agreements promotes the rights of all people to their lives, liberty, and property and helps to promote the common good.

Center for Civic Education

Content standards

1. **Interaction among nations.** *Students should be able to explain the major ways nations interact with one another.*

   To achieve this standard, students should be able to

   ■ explain how nations interact through

   - trade, e.g., buying and selling manufactured and agricultural goods such as airplanes, farm equipment, clothing, food

   - diplomacy, e.g., representatives of nations meeting, trying to find ways to solve problems peacefully

   - cultural contacts, e.g., international meetings of doctors, lawyers, oceanographers; tours of musical groups; exchanges of students and teachers; art exhibits

   - treaties or agreements, e.g., promises to defend one another, agreements to cooperate to protect the environment or to stop the drug trade

   - use of military force, e.g., World War II, Persian Gulf War

   ■ explain why it is important that nations try to resolve problems peacefully, e.g., promoting trade to improve peoples' standard of living, promoting peace to save human lives, protecting the environment, exchanging medical and scientific knowledge, exchanging students and teachers

   ■ explain the most important purposes of the U.N.

*We have a problem;
lets talk about it.*
John Maverick (1633)

*Center for Civic
Education*

V. WHAT ARE THE ROLES OF THE CITIZEN IN AMERICAN DEMOCRACY?

A. What does it mean to be a citizen of the United States?

Content summary and rationale

Citizenship in the United States means that a person is a legally recognized member of the nation. Each citizen has equal rights under the law. All citizens have certain rights, privileges, and responsibilities.

Americans who are not citizens have many of the same rights, privileges, and responsibilities of citizens. However, they do not have such important rights as the right to vote in elections, serve on juries, or hold elected office.

Content standards

1. **The meaning of citizenship.** *Students should be able to explain the meaning of citizenship in the United States.*

   To achieve this standard, students should be able to

   - explain the important characteristics of citizenship in the United States. Specifically, citizenship

     - means that a person is recognized as a legal member of the nation

     - gives each person certain rights and privileges, e.g., the right to vote and to hold public office

     - means each person has certain responsibilities, e.g., respecting the law, voting, paying taxes, serving on juries

   - explain that citizens owe allegiance or loyalty to the United States; in turn they receive protection and other services from the government

[T]he only title in our democracy superior to that of President [is] the title of citizen.

Louis Brandeis (c.1937)

B. How does a person become a citizen?

Content summary and rationale

Under current law, people who are born in the United States automatically become citizens, with few exceptions such as children of foreign diplomats. Adults who have come to the United States can apply to become citizens after residing in the country for five years, passing a test of their understanding of the United States Constitution and the history and government of the United States, and taking an oath of allegiance to the United States. Minors become citizens when their parents are naturalized.

Center for Civic Education

Content standards

1. **Becoming a citizen.** *Students should be able to explain how one becomes a citizen of the United States.*

   To achieve this standard, students should be able to

   ■ explain the difference between a citizen and a non-citizen (alien)

   ■ explain that people become citizens by birth or naturalization

C. What are important rights in the United States?

Content summary and rationale

One of the primary purposes of American government is the protection of personal, political, and economic rights of individuals. It is essential, therefore, for citizens to understand what these rights are and why they are important to themselves and their society.

Few, if any, rights can be considered absolute. Most rights may be limited when they conflict with other important rights, values, and interests. An understanding of both the importance of rights and the need for reasonable limitations upon them provides a basis for reasoned discussion of issues regarding them.

Content standards

1. **Rights of individuals.** *Students should be able to explain why certain rights are important to the individual and to a democratic society.*

   To achieve this standard, students should be able to

   ■ identify the following types of rights and explain their importance

   - **personal rights,** e.g., to associate with whomever one pleases, live where one chooses, practice the religion of one's choice, travel freely and return to the United States, emigrate

   - **political rights,** e.g., to vote, speak freely and criticize the government, join organizations that try to influence government policies, join a political party, seek and hold public office

   - **economic rights,** e.g., to own property, choose one's work, change employment, join a labor union, establish a business

   ■ identify contemporary issues regarding rights, e.g., school prayer, employment, welfare, equal pay for equal work

D. What are important responsibilities of Americans?

Content summary and rationale

An understanding of the importance of individual rights must be accompanied by an examination of personal and civic responsibilities. For American democracy to flourish, citizens not only must be aware of their rights, they must also exercise them responsibly and they must fulfill those responsibilities necessary to a self-governing, free, and just society.

Content standards

1. **Responsibilities of individuals.** *Students should be able to explain why certain responsibilities are important to themselves and their family, community, state, and nation.*

    To achieve this standard, students should be able to identify such responsibilities as the following and explain their importance

    ■ **personal responsibilities**, e.g., taking care of themselves, accepting responsibility for the consequences of their actions, taking advantage of the opportunity to be educated, supporting their families

    ■ **civic responsibilities**, e.g., obeying the law, respecting the rights of others, being informed and attentive to the needs of their community, paying attention to how well their elected leaders are doing their jobs, communicating with their representatives in their school, local, state, and national governments, voting, paying taxes, serving on juries, serving in the armed forces

No governmental action, no economic doctrine, no economic plan or project can replace that God-imposed responsibility of the individual man and woman to their neighbors.
Herbert Hoover (1931)

E. What dispositions or traits of character are important to the preservation and improvement of American democracy?

Content summary and rationale

Certain dispositions or traits of character not only help the individual become an effective and responsible participant in the political system, they contribute to the health of American democracy. These dispositions include traits of private character such as moral responsibility, self-discipline, respect for individual worth and human dignity, and compassion. They also include traits of public character such as civility, respect for law, civic mindedness, critical mindedness, persistence, and willingness to negotiate and compromise.

If students examine these dispositions, they may come to a deeper understanding of their importance.

Certain dispositions or traits of character not only help the individual become an effective and responsible participant in the political system, they contribute to the health of American democracy.

Content standards

1. **Dispositions that enhance citizen effectiveness and promote the healthy functioning of American democracy.** *Students should be able to explain the importance of certain dispositions to themselves and American democracy.*

    To achieve this standard, students should be able to

    ■ explain the importance of the following dispositions

    ▪ **individual responsibility**—fulfilling one's responsibilities to family, friends, and others in one's community and nation

    ▪ **self-discipline/self-governance**—obeying reasonable rules and laws voluntarily and not requiring others to force one to do so

    ▪ **civility**—treating other people with respect regardless of whether or not one likes them or agrees with their viewpoints, being willing to listen to other points of view, not being insulting when arguing with others

Civility costs nothing and buys everything.
Lady Mary Wortley Montagu
(1756)

Center for Civic Education

I say "try"; if we never try, we shall never succeed.

Abraham Lincoln (1862)

■ **respect** for the **rights of other individuals**—respect for the right of other people to hold and express their own opinions, respect for their right to a voice in their government

■ **honesty**—telling the truth

■ **respect for the law**—willingness to abide by laws, even though one may not be in complete agreement with every law

■ **open mindedness**—willingness to consider other points of view

■ **critical mindedness**—the inclination to question the truth of various positions, including one's own

■ **negotiation and compromise**—willingness to try to come to agreement with those with whom one may differ, when it is reasonable and morally justifiable

■ **persistence**—willingness to attempt again and again to accomplish a worthwhile goal

■ **civic mindedness**—concern for the well-being of one's community and nation

■ **compassion**—concern for the well-being of others, especially for the less fortunate

■ **patriotism**—loyalty to the values and principles underlying American constitutional democracy

If liberty and equality, as is thought by some, are chiefly to be found in democracy, they will be attained when all persons alike share in the government to the utmost.

Aristotle, Politics (c.340 B.C.)

F. How can Americans participate in their government?

Content summary and rationale

The well-being of American democracy depends upon the informed and effective participation of citizens concerned with the preservation of individual rights and the promotion of the common good. Americans have always engaged in cooperative action for common purposes. Participation in government, contrasted with the wider realm of organized social participation, has ebbed in recent decades, however. Indifference to or alienation from politics may characterize a significant segment of the population.

If citizens want their views to be considered, they must become active participants in the political process. Although elections, campaigns, and voting are at the center of democratic institutions, citizens should be aware of the many other participatory opportunities available to them. These possibilities include becoming informed about political issues, discussing public issues, contacting public officials, and joining interest groups and political parties.

If citizens want their views to be considered, they must become active participants in the political process.

Content standards

1. **Forms of participation.** *Students should be able to describe the means by which citizens can influence the decisions and actions of their government.*

   To achieve this standard, students should be able to

   ■ identify ways people can monitor and influence the decisions and actions of their government

      ■ reading about public issues, watching television news programs

Center for Civic Education

- discussing public issues
- communicating with public officials
- voting
- taking an active role in interest groups, political parties, and other organizations that attempt to influence public policy and elections
- attending meetings of governing agencies e.g., city council, school board
- working in campaigns
- circulating and signing petitions
- taking part in peaceful demonstrations
- contributing money to political parties, candidates or causes

■ identify individuals or groups who monitor and influence the decisions and actions of their local, state, tribal, and national governments, e.g., the media, labor unions, P.T.A., Chamber of Commerce, taxpayer associations, civilian review boards

■ explain why it is important for citizens to monitor their local, state and national governments

Where everyman is...participator in the government of affairs, not merely at an election one day in the year but every day...he will let the heart be torn out of his body sooner than his power be wrested from him by a Caesar or a Bonaparte.
Thomas Jefferson (1816)

G. What is the importance of political leadership and public service?

Content summary and rationale

Political leadership and careers in public service are vitally important in the American democracy. Citizens need to understand what political leaders do and why leadership is necessary. They also must understand the wide range of positions and opportunities in public service and their importance to themselves and their society.

Content standards

1. **Political leadership and public service.** *Students should be able to explain the importance of political leadership and public service in their school, community, state, and nation.*

   To achieve this standard, students should be able to

   ■ describe what political leaders do and why leadership is necessary in a democracy

   ■ identify opportunities for leadership and public service in their own classroom, school, community, state, and nation

   ■ explain the importance of individuals working cooperatively with their elected leaders

   ■ explain why leadership and public service are important to the continuance and improvement of American democracy

I am only one; but still I am one. I cannot do everything, but still I can do something; I will not refuse to do the something I can do.
Helen Keller (c.1950)

Center for Civic Education

H. How should Americans select leaders?

Content summary and rationale

Citizens need to learn how to examine the responsibilities of differing positions of authority and how to evaluate the qualifications of candidates for those positions. The development among citizens of the capacity to select competent and responsible persons to fill positions of leadership in American government is essential to the well-being of the nation.

Content standards

1. **Selecting leaders.** *Students should be able to explain and apply criteria useful in selecting leaders in their school, community, state, and nation*

   To achieve this standard, students should be able to

   - identify the major duties, powers, privileges, and limitations of a position of leadership, e.g., class president, mayor, state senator, tribal chairperson, president of the United States
   - identify qualities leaders should have such as
     - commitment to the values and principles of constitutional democracy
     - respect for the rights of others
     - ability to work with others
     - reliability or dependability
     - courage
     - honesty
     - ability to be fair
     - intelligence
     - willingness to work hard
     - special knowledge or skills
   - evaluate the strengths and weaknesses of candidates in terms of the qualifications required for a particular leadership role

Stand with anybody that stands right. Stand with him while he is right, and part with him when he goes wrong.

Abraham Lincoln (1854)

Center for Civic Education

5-8 Content Standards

5-8 Content Standards

I. WHAT ARE CIVIC LIFE, POLITICS, AND GOVERNMENT?

A. What is civic life? What is politics? What is government? Why are government and politics necessary? What purposes should government serve?

Content summary and rationale

Civic life is the public life of the citizen concerned with the affairs of the community and nation, as contrasted with private or personal life, which is devoted to the pursuit of private and personal interests.

Politics is a process by which a group of people, whose opinions or interests may be divergent, reach collective decisions that are generally regarded as binding on the group and enforced as common policy. Every social group, including the family, schools, labor unions, and professional organizations, is engaged in politics, in its broadest sense. Politics is an inescapable activity, and political life enables people to accomplish goals they could not realize as individuals.

Government is the people and institutions in a society with authority to make, carry out, enforce laws, and settle disputes about law that, in general, deal with the distribution of resources in a society, the allocation of benefits and burdens, and the management of conflict.

Differing assumptions about the proper relationship between civic and private life influence ideas about the purposes of government. Differing ideas about the purposes of government have profound consequences for the well-being of individuals and society. For example, if one believes that the activities of government should be restricted to providing for the security of the lives and property of citizens, one might believe in placing severe restrictions on the right of government to intrude into their private or personal lives. On the other hand, if one believes that the moral character of the individual should be a public or civic matter, one might support a broad range of laws and regulations concerning private behavior and belief.

Citizens need to understand competing ideas about civic life, politics, and government so that they can make informed judgments about what their government should and should not do, about how they are to live their lives together, and about how to support the proper use of authority and combat the abuse of political power.

> *Politics is a process by which a group of people, whose opinions or interests may be divergent, reach collective decisions that are generally regarded as binding on the group and enforced as common policy. Every social group...is engaged in politics.*

Content standards

1. **Defining civic life, politics, and government.** *Students should be able to explain the meaning of the terms civic life, politics, and government.*

    To achieve this standard, students should be able to

    ■ define and distinguish between private life and civic life

        ■ **private life** concerns the personal life of the individual, e.g, being with family and friends, joining clubs or teams, practicing one's religious beliefs, earning money

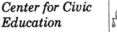

- **civic life** concerns taking part in the governance of the school, community, tribe, state, or nation, e.g., helping to find solutions to problems, helping to make rules and laws, serving as elected leaders

- describe **politics** as the ways people whose ideas may differ reach agreements that are generally regarded as binding on the group, e.g., presenting information and evidence, stating arguments, negotiating, compromising, voting

- describe **government** as the people and institutions with authority to make, carry out, enforce laws, and manage disputes about law

  - define authority as the right, legitimized by custom, law, consent, or principles of morality, to use power to direct or control people

  - identify institutions with authority to direct or control the behavior of members of a society, e.g., a school board, city council, state legislature, courts, Congress

  - define power without authority as power that is not legitimized by custom, law, consent, or principles of morality

  - identify examples of the exercise of power without authority, e.g., a street gang, a military junta, a self-proclaimed dictatorship

2. **Necessity and purposes of government.** *Students should be able to evaluate, take, and defend positions on why government is necessary and the purposes government should serve.*

To achieve this standard, students should be able to

- explain major ideas about why government is necessary, e.g.,

  - people's lives, liberty, and property would be insecure without government, e.g., there would be no laws to control people's behavior, the strong might take advantage of the weak

  - individuals by themselves cannot do many of the things they can do collectively, e.g., create a system of highways, provide armed forces for the security of the nation, make and enforce laws

- evaluate competing ideas about the purposes government should serve, e.g.,

  - protecting individual rights

  - promoting the common good

  - providing economic security

  - molding the character of citizens

  - furthering the interests of a particular class or group

  - promoting a particular religion

[Without government:] No arts; no letters; no society; and which is worst of all, continual fear and danger of violent death; and the life of man, solitary, poor, nasty, brutish, and short.

Thomas Hobbes (1651)

Center for Civic Education

B. What are the essential characteristics of limited and unlimited government?

Content summary and rationale

Limited government provides a basis for protecting individual rights and promoting the common good in contrast to **unlimited government** which endangers these values. Limited government is constitutional government. Unlimited governments include authoritarian and totalitarian systems.

The **rule of law** is an essential component of limited government. The central notion of a rule of law is that society is governed according to widely known and accepted rules followed not only by the governed but also by those in authority.

Civil society is that sphere of voluntary individual, social, and economic relationships and organizations that, although limited by law, is not part of governmental institutions. Civil society provides a domain where individuals are free from unreasonable interference from government. By providing for independent centers of power and influence, civil society is an indispensable means of maintaining limited government.

Civil society provides a domain where individuals are free from unreasonable interference from government.

An understanding of the concept of limited government and its essential components helps citizens understand the necessity of maintaining those conditions that prevent a particular government from exceeding its powers.

An awareness of different types of limited governments provides citizens with a basis for making reasoned judgments about proposals to alter their own government and for evaluating the governments of other nations.

Content standards

1. **Limited and unlimited governments**. *Students should be able to describe the essential characteristics of limited and unlimited governments.*

   To achieve this standard, students should be able to

   - describe the essential characteristics of limited and unlimited governments

     - limited governments have established and respected restraints on their power, e.g.,

       - constitutional governments—governments characterized by legal limits on political power

     - unlimited governments are those in which there are no effective means of restraining their power, e.g.

       - authoritarian systems—governments in which political power is concentrated in one person or a small group, and individuals and groups are subordinated to that power

       - totalitarian systems—modern forms of extreme authoritarianism in which the government attempts to control every aspect of the lives of individuals and prohibits independent associations

No freeman shall be taken, or imprisoned, or outlawed, or exiled, or in any way harmed...except by the legal judgment of his peers or by the law of the land.
Magna Carta (1215)

Center for Civic Education

Power tends to corrupt and absolute power corrupts absolutely.
Lord Acton (1887)

■ identify historical and contemporary examples of limited and unlimited governments and justify their classification, e.g.,

■ limited governments—United States, Great Britain, Botswana, Japan, Israel, Chile

■ unlimited governments—Nazi Germany, Imperial Japan, Spain under Franco, Argentina under Peron, Iraq under Hussein, Iran

2. **The rule of law.** *Students should be able to explain the importance of the rule of law for the protection of individual rights and the common good.*

To achieve this standard, students should be able to

■ explain the difference between the rule of law and the "rule of men"

■ explain how the rule of law can be used to restrict the actions of private citizens and government officials alike in order to protect the rights of individuals and to promote the common good

Wherever Law ends, Tyranny begins.
John Locke (1690)

■ explain the consequences of the absence of a rule of law, e.g.,

■ anarchy

■ arbitrary and capricious rule

■ absence of predictability

■ disregard for established and fair procedures

C. What are the nature and purposes of constitutions?

Content summary and rationale

The term **"constitution"** has alternative meanings, and constitutions serve differing purposes in different nations. In some nations a constitution is only a description of a form of government. In the United States, as well as in some other nations, a constitution is a form of **higher law** that **establishes** the powers of government and **limits** them in order to protect individual rights as well as to promote the common good. In some nations with unlimited governments, constitutions have served as a cloak to misrule, disguising the unconstrained behavior of rulers.

Though written constitutions may be violated in moments of passion or delusion, yet they furnish a text to which those who are watchful may again rally and recall the people; they fix too for the people the principles of their political creed.
Thomas Jefferson (1802)

In the United States, **constitutional government** is equated with limited government. Even in a constitutional government, however, the constitution alone cannot guarantee that the limits imposed on government will be respected or that the purposes of government will be served. There are certain social, economic, and political conditions that enable constitutional government to flourish.

To preserve and improve constitutional government, citizens must understand the conditions necessary for its existence. There must be general agreement about the proper relationship among the people, their constitution, and their government. Finally, not only must a constitution regulate institutions, the people also must cultivate a disposition to behave in ways consistent with its values and principles.

Content standards

1. **Concepts of "constitution."** *Students should be able to explain alternative uses of the term "constitution" and to distinguish between governments with a constitution and a constitutional government.*

   To achieve this standard, students should be able to

   - distinguish among the following uses of the term constitution

     - constitution as a description of a form of government

     - constitution as a document

     - constitution as a higher law limiting the powers of government, i.e., a constitutional or limited government

   - identify historical and contemporary nations with constitutions that in reality do not limit power, e.g., former Soviet Union, Nazi Germany, Iraq under Saddam Hussein

   - identify historical and contemporary nations with constitutions that in reality do limit power, e.g., United States, United Kingdom, Germany, Japan, Botswana, Chile

   - explain that a government with a constitution but with no effective ways to enforce its limitations is not a constitutional government

2. **Purposes and uses of constitutions.** *Students should be able to explain the various purposes constitutions serve.*

   To achieve this standard, students should be able to

   - explain how constitutions

     - set forth the purposes of government

     - describe the way a government is organized and how power is allocated

     - define the relationship between a people and their government

   - describe historical and contemporary examples of how constitutions have been used to promote the interests of a particular group, class, religion, or political party, e.g., the People's Republic of China, Kenya, Mexico

   - describe historical and contemporary examples of how constitutions have been used to protect individual rights and promote the common good, e.g., United States Constitution "Congress shall make no law respecting an establishment of religion, (First Amendment) ...," "The right of citizens of the United States to vote shall not be denied...on account of sex (Nineteenth Amendment)."

Articles 114, 115, 117, 118, 123, 124 and 153 of the constitution of the German Reich are cancelled until further notice. This allows certain restrictions to be imposed on personal freedom, on the right to express a free opinion, the freedom of the press, of association and the right to hold meetings, it allows restrictions on the secrecy of the mail, post and telecommunications systems, the ordering of house searches and confiscation of property and restrictions on property rights.
Decree of the Reich President (1933)

In the United States, as well as in some other nations, a constitution is a form of higher law that establishes and limits government in order to protect individual rights as well as to promote the common good.

Center for Civic Education

A popular government without popular information or the means of acquiring it is but a prologue to Farce or Tragedy or perhaps both. Knowledge will forever govern ignorance, and a people who mean to be their own Governors must arm themselves with the power knowledge gives.

James Madison (1788)

3. **Conditions under which constitutional government flourishes.** *Students should be able to explain those conditions that are essential for the flourishing of constitutional government.*

To achieve this standard, students should be able to

■ explain the importance of establishing and maintaining conditions that help constitutional government to flourish such as

   ■ a citizenry that

      ■ is educated and enjoys a reasonable standard of living

      ■ understands and supports the constitution and its values and principles

      ■ willingly assumes the responsibilities of citizenship

      ■ insists that government officials respect limitations the constitution places on their authority

   ■ persons serving in government who

      ■ understand and support the constitution and its values and principles

      ■ respect limitations the constitution places on their authority

D. What are alternative ways of organizing constitutional governments?

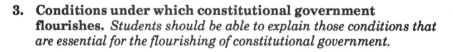

Content summary and rationale

The way a government is organized is a reflection of its most fundamental purposes. For that reason, constitutional governments organize their institutions to channel and limit the exercise of political power to serve the purposes for which they have been established.

The way a government is organized is a reflection of its most fundamental purposes.

The most common forms of organization of the institutions of central governments at the national level are **systems of shared powers** and **parliamentary systems**.

■ In **systems of shared powers**, such as the United States, powers are separated among branches, each of which has primary responsibility for certain functions, but each branch also shares these powers and functions with other branches, e.g., the president, Congress, and the Supreme Court all share power regarding the laws of the nation.

■ In **parliamentary systems** such as Great Britain, authority is held by a bicameral legislature called Parliament. Parliament consists of the House of Lords and the House of Commons. The prime minister is chosen by convention from the ranks of the majority party in Commons. The prime minister forms a cabinet and directs the administration of the government.

There are several kinds of relationships between the central government of a nation and other units of government within the nation. The most common forms of such relationships, all of which have been or can be found in the United States, are **confederal, federal, and unitary systems**.

By comparing alternative means of organizing constitutional governments, citizens become aware of the advantages and disadvantages of their own system and how it may be improved. This understanding also provides a basis for evaluating whether one's own government is diverging from its constitutional design and purposes. This knowledge not only helps citizens to understand their own government, it also enables them to grasp the meaning of events in the world, such as the fall of parliamentary governments, the breakup of federations, or the weaknesses of confederations.

Content standards

1. **Shared powers and parliamentary systems.** *Students should be able to describe the major characteristics of systems of shared powers and of parliamentary systems.*

   To achieve this standard, students should be able to

   - describe the major characteristics of systems of shared powers, e.g., in the United States

     - the president and members of the Cabinet cannot be members of Congress

     - powers are separated among branches, each branch has primary responsibility for certain functions, e.g., legislative, executive, and judicial

     - each branch also shares the powers and functions of the other branches, e.g.,

       - Congress may pass laws, but the president may veto them

       - the president nominates certain public officials, but the Senate needs to approve them

       - Congress may pass laws, but the Supreme Court may declare them unconstitutional

   - describe the major characteristics of parliamentary systems, e.g., in the United Kingdom

     - authority is held by a legislature called Parliament

     - the political party or parties that can form a majority in Parliament choose the prime minister

     - the prime minister chooses members of Parliament to serve in the cabinet

     - the prime minister and members of the cabinet must all be members of the legislature—Parliament

     - the prime minister and cabinet direct the administration of the government

     - the prime minister and cabinet may be replaced by Parliament if a majority vote "no confidence" in the government

By comparing alternative means of organizing constitutional governments, citizens become aware of the advantages and disadvantages of their own system and how it may be improved.

Each state retains its sovereignty, freedom, and independence and every Power, Jurisdiction and right, which is not by this confederation expressly delegated to the United States, in Congress assembled.

Articles of Confederation (1781)

2. **Confederal, federal, and unitary systems.** *Students should be able to explain the advantages and disadvantages of confederal, federal, and unitary systems of government.*

   To achieve this standard, students should be able to

   ■ define confederal, federal, and unitary systems of government

      ■ confederal system—a system of government in which sovereign states delegate powers to a national government for specific purposes

      ■ federal system—a system in which power is divided and shared between national and state governments

      ■ unitary system—a system in which all power is concentrated in a central government; state and local governments can exercise only those powers given to them by the central government

   ■ identify examples of confederal, federal, and unitary systems in the history of the United States, e.g,

      ■ confederal system—the United States under the Articles of Confederation and the Confederate States of America

      ■ federal system—the government of the United States

      ■ unitary system—state governments of the United States

   ■ explain the major advantages and disadvantages of confederal, federal, and unitary systems

II. WHAT ARE THE FOUNDATIONS OF THE AMERICAN POLITICAL SYSTEM?

A. What is the American idea of constitutional government?

Content summary and rationale

Using a written constitution to set forth the values and principles of government and to establish and limit its powers is among this nation's most distinctive accomplishments. The American system of government relies on its citizens' commitment to these constitutional values and principles set forth in the Constitution, as well as in the Declaration of Independence and other writings. These values and principles provide the foundation for the establishment, in James Madison's words, of an "energetic" and effective government, one capable of fulfilling the purposes for which it was created—to protect the inalienable rights of the individual to life, liberty, and property and to promote the common good.

But an equally important purpose of the Constitution is to separate and limit the powers of government so that the basic liberties of the people are not infringed. The Bill of Rights was added to the Constitution to clarify and strengthen limitations on the powers of the national government, and it has become central to the American idea of constitutional government.

Citizens must understand the importance of the fundamental ideas of American constitutional government to develop a reasoned commitment to them, as well as to use them as criteria to evaluate their own behavior and the behavior of government officials.

Content standards

1. **The American idea of constitutional government.** *Students should be able to explain the essential ideas of American constitutional government.*

   To achieve this standard, students should be able to

   ■ explain essential ideas of American constitutional government as expressed in the Declaration of Independence, the Constitution, and other writings, e.g.,

     ■ the people are sovereign; they are the ultimate source of power

     ■ the Constitution is a higher law that authorizes a government of limited powers

     ■ the purposes of government, as stated in the Preamble to the Constitution, are to

       ■ form a more perfect union

       ■ establish justice

       ■ insure domestic tranquility

       ■ provide for the common defense

       ■ promote the general welfare

       ■ secure the blessings of liberty to ourselves and our posterity

Using a written constitution to set forth the values and principles of government and to establish and limit its powers is among this nation's most distinctive accomplishments.

[The government of the United States is] a government limited...by the authority of a paramount Constitution.
James Madison (1788)

The people made the Constitution, and the people can unmake it. It is the creature of their own will, and lives only by their will.
John Marshall (1821)

[I]nterpreted as it ought to be interpreted, the Constitution is a GLORIOUS LIBERTY DOCUMENT.
Frederick Douglass (1852)

It was from America that...ideas long locked in the breast of solitary thinkers, and hidden among Latin folios—burst forth like a conqueror upon the world... and the principle gained ground, that a nation can never abandon its fate to an authority it cannot control.

Lord Acton (1907)

Liberty cannot live apart from constitutional principle.

Woodrow Wilson (1887)

- explain how the following provisions of the United States Constitution give government the power it needs to fulfill the purposes for which it was established

  - **delegated or enumerated powers**, e.g., to lay and collect taxes, to make treaties, to decide cases and controversies between two or more states (Articles I, II & III)
  - **the general welfare provision** (Article I, Section 8)
  - **the necessary and proper clause** (Article I, Section 8, Clause 18)

- explain the means of limiting the powers of government under the United States Constitution

  - separation and sharing of powers
  - checks and balances
  - Bill of Rights

- explain how specific provisions of the United States Constitution, including the Bill of Rights, limit the powers of government in order to protect the rights of individuals, e.g., habeas corpus; trial by jury; ex post facto; freedom of religion, speech, press, and assembly; equal protection of the law; due process of law; right to counsel

- evaluate, take, and defend positions on current issues involving constitutional protection of individual rights, such as

  - limits on speech, e.g., "hate speech," advertising, libel and slander, "fighting words"
  - separation of church and state, e.g., school vouchers, prayer in public schools
  - cruel and unusual punishment, e.g., death penalty
  - search and seizure, e.g., warrantless searches
  - privacy, e.g., fingerprinting of children, national identification cards, wiretapping, DNA banks

B. What are the distinctive characteristics of American society?

Content summary and rationale

The distinctive characteristics of American society have shaped Americans' ideas about the proper relationship among individuals, society, and the government.

The distinctive characteristics of American society have shaped Americans' ideas about the proper relationship among individuals, society, and the government. Americans need to understand these characteristics in order to know who they are—their identity as a people. This understanding of a common identity and common purposes provides a basis on which American society can work cooperatively to solve common problems and manage conflicts within constitutional boundaries.

Unlike many other nations, the United States never experienced feudalism, accepted an inherited caste system, or recognized a nobility. The existence of a frontier, large-scale and continuing immigration, and the abundance and widespread ownership of property, have fostered the growth of a democratic way of life. Notable exceptions that have worked against the attainment of social equality are the history of slavery, the treatment of Native Americans, and discrimination against various groups.

A belief in social equality and a democratic way of life has fostered voluntarism, another prominent characteristic of Americans. The American tradition of voluntarism emerged from the colonists' dependence on one another during the early settlement period, was enhanced by the influence of a frontier, and was encouraged by Americans' religious beliefs. This propensity for voluntarism has continued to the present day and has given rise to questions that citizens need to address: Is it advantageous for society that certain functions, such as education and social welfare, be performed by voluntary associations? By government? Or should both have a role? Would American society be harmed if the propensity to voluntarism declined?

Recognition of the many forms of diversity in American society—ethnicity, race, religion, class, language, gender, or national origin—embraced in a constitutional system, is a prerequisite to making judgments about the benefits diversity offers and the challenges it poses.

A belief in social equality and a democratic way of life have fostered voluntarism, another prominent characteristic of Americans.

Content standards

1. **Distinctive characteristics of American society.** *Students should be able to identify and explain the importance of historical experience and geographic, social, and economic factors that have helped to shape American society.*

   To achieve this standard, students should be able to

   - explain important factors that have helped shape American society

     - absence of a nobility or an inherited caste system
     - religious freedom
     - the Judeo-Christian ethic
     - a history of slavery
     - relative geographic isolation
     - abundance of land and widespread ownership of property
     - social, economic, and geographic mobility
     - effects of a frontier
     - large scale immigration
     - diversity of the population
     - individualism
     - work ethic
     - market economy
     - relative social equality
     - universal public education

Democracy is still upon its trial. The civic genius of our people is its only bulwark.
William James (1897)

2. **The role of voluntarism in American life.** *Students should be able to evaluate, take, and defend positions on the importance of voluntarism in American society.*

   To achieve this standard, students should be able to

   - explain factors that have inclined Americans toward voluntarism, e.g., colonial conditions, frontier traditions, religious beliefs

I come of Quaker stock. My ancestors were persecuted for their beliefs. Here they sought and found religious freedom. By blood and conviction I stand for religious tolerance both in act and in spirit.
Herbert Hoover (1928)

Center for Civic Education

The one absolutely certain way of bringing this nation to ruin, of preventing all possibility of its continuing to be a nation at all would be to permit it to become a tangle of squabbling nationalities... each preserving its separate nationality.

Theodore Roosevelt (1910)

■ identify services that religious, charitable, and civic groups provide in their own community, e.g., health, child, and elderly care; disaster relief; counseling; tutoring; basic needs such as food, clothing, shelter

■ identify opportunities for individuals to volunteer in their own schools and communities

3. **Diversity in American society.** *Students should be able to evaluate, take, and defend positions on the value and challenges of diversity in American life.*

To achieve this standard, students should be able to

■ identify the many forms of diversity in American society, e.g., regional, linguistic, racial, religious, ethnic, socioeconomic

■ explain why diversity is desirable and beneficial, e.g., increases choice, fosters a variety of viewpoints, encourages cultural creativity

■ explain why conflicts have arisen from diversity, using historical and contemporary examples, e.g., North/South conflict; conflict about land, suffrage, and other rights of Native Americans; Catholic/Protestant conflicts in the nineteenth century; conflict about civil rights of minorities and women; present day ethnic conflict in urban settings

■ evaluate ways conflicts about diversity can be resolved in a peaceful manner that respects individual rights and promotes the common good

C. What is American political culture?

The principle on which this country was founded and by which it has always been governed is that Americanism is a matter of the mind and heart; Americanism is not, and never was, a matter of race and ancestry. A good American is one who is loyal to this country and to our creed of liberty and democracy.

Franklin Delano Roosevelt (1943)

Content Summary and Rationale

In contrast to most other nations, the identity of an American is defined by shared political values and principles rather than by ethnicity, race, religion, class, language, gender, or national origin. These shared values and principles have helped to promote cohesion in the daily life of Americans and in times of crisis have enabled them to find common ground with those who differ from them.

While political conflicts sometimes have erupted in violence—labor disputes, race riots, and draft riots—citizens should understand that political conflict in the United States has usually been less divisive and violent than in other nations. This is because American political conflict, with the major exception of the Civil War, labor unrest, civil rights struggles, and the opposition to the war in Vietnam, has generally taken place within a constitutional framework which allows for protest politics and promotes the peaceful resolution of differences.

To understand their nation, citizens should appreciate the nature of American political culture, which provides a foundation for the stability of the system of government and its capacity to respond to the needs and interests of the people through peaceful change.

Content standards

1. **American identity.** *Students should be able to explain the importance of shared political values and principles to American society.*

   To achieve this standard, students should be able to

   - explain that an American's identity stems from belief in and allegiance to shared political values and principles rather than from ethnicity, race, religion, class, language, gender, or national origin, which determine identity in most other nations

   - identify basic values and principles Americans share as set forth in such documents as the Declaration of Independence, the United States Constitution, the Gettysburg Address

   - explain why it is important to the individual and society that Americans understand and act on their shared political values and principles

2. **The character of American political conflict.** *Students should be able to describe the character of American political conflict and explain factors that usually prevent violence or that lower its intensity.*

   To achieve this standard, students should be able to

   - describe political conflict in the United States both historically and at present, such as conflict about

     - geographic and sectional interests

     - slavery and indentured servitude

     - national origins

     - extending the franchise

     - extending civil rights to all Americans

     - the role of religion in American public life

     - engaging in wars

   - explain some of the reasons why political conflict in the United States, with notable exceptions such as the Civil War, labor unrest, civil rights struggles, and the opposition to the war in Vietnam generally has been less divisive than in many other nations. These include

     - a shared respect for the Constitution and its principles

     - a sense of unity within diversity

     - many opportunities to influence government and to participate in it

     - willingness to relinquish power when voted out of office

     - acceptance of the idea of majority rule tempered by a respect for minority rights

     - willingness to use the legal system to manage conflicts

     - availability of land and abundance of natural resources

     - a relatively high standard of living

     - opportunities to improve one's economic condition

     - opportunities for free, public education

We march in the name of the Constitution, knowing that the Constitution is on our side. The right of the people peaceably to assemble and to petition the Government for a redress of grievances shall not be abridged. That's the First Amendment.

Martin Luther King, Jr.
(c.1963)

Center for Civic Education

The Spirit that prevails among Men of all degrees, all ages and sexes is the Spirit of Liberty.
Abigail Adams (1775)

We hold these Truths to be self-evident, that all Men are created equal, that they are endowed by their Creator with certain unalienable Rights, that among these are Life, Liberty, and the Pursuit of Happiness—That to secure these Rights, Governments are instituted among Men, deriving their just Powers from the Consent of the Governed....
Declaration of Independence (1776)

I have never had a feeling, politically, that did not spring from the sentiments embodied in the Declaration of Independence.
Abraham Lincoln (1861)

D. What values and principles are basic to American constitutional democracy?

Content summary and rationale

Agreement on certain fundamental values and principles is essential to the preservation and improvement of American constitutional democracy. They are stated in the Declaration of Independence, the Constitution, the Gettysburg Address, and other significant documents, speeches and writings. They provide common ground on which Americans can work together to decide how best to promote the attainment of individual, community, and national goals.

The values and principles of American constitutional democracy have shaped the nation's political institutions and practices. These values and principles are sometimes in conflict, however, and their very meaning and application are often disputed. For example, although most Americans agree that the idea of equality is an important value, they may disagree about what priority it should be given in comparison with other values, such as liberty. They also may disagree on the meaning of equality when it is applied to a specific situation. To participate constructively in public debate concerning fundamental values and principles, citizens need a sufficient understanding of them.

Disparities have always existed between the realities of daily life and the ideals of American constitutional democracy. The history of the United States, however, has been marked by continuing attempts to narrow the gap between ideals and reality. For these reasons, Americans have joined forces in political movements to abolish slavery, extend the franchise, remove legal support for segregation, and provide equality of opportunity for each individual. Citizens need to be aware of historical and contemporary efforts of Americans who, through individual, social, and political action, have sought to lessen the disparity between ideals and reality. Citizens need to understand that American society is perpetually "unfinished," and that each generation has an obligation to help the nation move closer to the realization of its ideals.

Content standards

1. **Fundamental values and principles.** *Students should be able to explain the meaning and importance of the fundamental values and principles of American constitutional democracy.*

   To achieve this standard, students should be able to

   ■ identify fundamental values and principles as expressed in

     ■ basic documents, e.g., Declaration of Independence and United States Constitution

     ■ significant political speeches and writings, e.g., *The Federalist*, Washington's Farewell Address, Lincoln's Gettysburg Address, King's "I Have a Dream" speech

     ■ individual and group actions that embody fundamental values and principles, e.g., suffrage and civil rights movements

Center for Civic Education

- explain the meaning and importance of each of the following values considered to be fundamental to American public life

  - individual rights: life, liberty, property, and the pursuit of happiness

  - the common or public good

  - self government

  - justice

  - equality

  - diversity

  - openness and free inquiry

  - truth

  - patriotism

- explain the meaning and importance of the following fundamental principles of American constitutional democracy

  - **popular sovereignty**—the concept that ultimate political authority rests with the people who create and can alter or abolish governments

  - **constitutional government** which includes

    - the rule of law

    - representative institutions

    - shared powers

    - checks and balances

    - individual rights

    - separation of church and state

    - federalism

    - civilian control of the military

2. **Conflicts among values and principles in American political and social life.** *Students should be able to evaluate, take, and defend positions on issues in which fundamental values and principles are in conflict.*

To achieve this standard, students should be able to

- describe conflicts among fundamental values and principles and give historical and contemporary examples of these conflicts, such as

  - conflicts between liberty and equality, e.g., liberty to exclude others from private clubs and the right of individuals to be treated equally

  - conflicts between individual rights and the common good, e.g., liberty to smoke in public places and protection of the health of other persons

- explain why people may agree on values or principles in the abstract but disagree when they are applied to specific issues

America has always been about rights.... While many nations are based on a shared language or ethnic heritage, Americans have made rights the foundation of their national identity.
J. Jackson Barlow (1987)

The way to secure liberty is to place it in the people's hands, that is, to give them the power at all times to defend it in the legislature and in the courts of justice.
John Adams (1787)

I have a dream that my four little children will one day live in a nation where they will not be judged by the color of their skin but by the content of their character.
Martin Luther King, Jr.
(1963)

Center for Civic Education

Here, in the first paragraph of the Declaration [of Independence], is the assertion of the natural right of all to the ballot; for how can "the consent of the governed" be given, if the right to vote be denied?
Susan B. Anthony (1873)

- agreement on the value of freedom of expression but disagreement about the extent to which expression of unpopular and offensive views should be tolerated, e.g., neo-Nazi demonstrations, racial slurs, profanity, lyrics that advocate violence

- agreement on the value of equality but disagreement about affirmative action programs

3. **Disparities between ideals and reality in American political and social life.** *Students should be able to evaluate, take, and defend positions on issues concerning ways and means to reduce disparities between American ideals and realities.*

To achieve this standard, students should be able to

- identify some important American ideals, e.g., liberty and justice for all, an informed citizenry, civic virtue or concern for the common good, respect for the rights of others

- explain the importance of ideals as goals, even if they are not fully achieved

- explain, using historical and contemporary examples, discrepancies between American ideals and the realities of political and social life in the United States, e.g., the ideal of equal justice for all and the reality that the poor may not have equal access to the judicial system.

- describe historical and contemporary efforts to reduce discrepancies between ideals and the reality of American public life, e.g., abolition, suffrage, civil rights, and environmental protection movements

- explain ways in which discrepancies between reality and the ideals of American constitutional democracy can be reduced by

  - individual action

  - social action

  - political action

Let me be a free man—free to travel, free to stop, free to work, free to trade where I choose, free to choose my own teachers, free to follow the religion of my fathers, free to think and talk and act for myself— and I will obey every law, or submit to the penalty.
Chief Joseph (1879)

III. HOW DOES THE GOVERNMENT ESTABLISHED BY THE CONSTITUTION EMBODY THE PURPOSES, VALUES, AND PRINCIPLES OF AMERICAN DEMOCRACY?

A. How are power and responsibility distributed, shared, and limited in the government established by the United States Constitution?

Content summary and rationale

The system of government established by the Constitution has resulted in a complex dispersal of powers. As a result, every American lives under the jurisdiction of national, state, and local governments, all of whose powers and responsibilities are separated and shared among different branches and agencies.

All these governments—national, state, and local—affect the daily life of every American. This complex system of multiple levels and divisions of government is difficult to understand and is sometimes inefficient. It may result in delaying or preventing action by government which may or may not be desirable. The Framers of the Constitution saw this system as a principal means of limiting the power of government. It provides numerous opportunities for citizens to participate in their own governance. It reflects the principle of popular sovereignty, enables citizens to hold their governments accountable, and helps to insure protection for the rights of the people.

Citizens who understand the reasons for this system of dispersed power and its design are able to evaluate, monitor, and influence it more effectively.

Americans live under the jurisdiction of national, state, and local governments.

Content standards

1. **Distributing, sharing, and limiting powers of the national government.** *Students should be able to explain how the powers of the national government are distributed, shared, and limited.*

   To achieve this standard, students should be able to

   ■ explain how the three opening words of the Preamble to the Constitution, "We the People...," embody the principle of the people as sovereign—the ultimate source of authority

   ■ explain how legislative, executive, and judicial powers are distributed and shared among the three branches of the national government

     ■ legislative power—although primary legislative power lies with Congress, it is shared with the other branches, e.g., the executive branch can submit bills for consideration and can establish regulations, the Supreme Court can interpret laws and can declare them unconstitutional

     ■ executive power—although primary executive power is with the executive branch, it is shared by the other branches, e.g., congressional committees have authority to review actions of the executive branch, the Senate must approve appointments and ratify treaties, the Supreme Court can review actions of the executive branch and declare them unconstitutional

The power vested in the American courts of justice of pronouncing a statute to be unconstitutional forms one of the most powerful barriers that have ever been devised against the tyranny of political assemblies.
Alexis de Tocqueville (1835)

Center for Civic Education

- judicial power—although primary judicial power is with the federal judiciary, it is shared with other branches, e.g., the president appoints federal judges, the Senate can approve or refuse to confirm federal court appointees, the executive branch can hold administrative hearings on compliance with regulations and laws, Congress can "overturn" a Supreme Court interpretation of a law by amending it

- explain how each branch of government can check the powers of the other branches

  - legislative branch has the power to

    - establish committees to oversee activities of the executive branch

    - impeach the president, other members of the executive branch, and federal judges

    - pass laws over the president's veto by two-thirds majority vote of both Houses

    - disapprove appointments made by the president

    - propose amendments to the United States Constitution

  - executive branch has the power to

    - veto laws passed by Congress

    - nominate members of the federal judiciary

  - judicial branch has the power to

    - overrule decisions made by lower courts

    - declare laws made by Congress to be unconstitutional

    - declare actions of the executive branch to be unconstitutional

2. **Sharing of powers between the national and state governments.** *Students should be able to explain how and why powers are distributed and shared between national and state governments in the federal system.*

To achieve this standard, students should be able to

- identify the major parts of the federal system

  - national government

  - state governments

  - other governmental units, e.g., District of Columbia; American tribal governments; territories of Puerto Rico, Guam, American Samoa; Virgin Islands

- describe how some powers are shared between the national and state governments, e.g., power to tax, borrow money, regulate voting

- describe functions commonly and primarily exercised by state governments, e.g., education, law enforcement, health and hospitals, roads and highways

- identify powers prohibited to state governments by the United States Constitution, e.g., coining money, conducting foreign relations, interfering with interstate commerce, raising an army and declaring war (Article I, Section 10)

The proposed Constitution, so far from implying an abolition of the State Governments, makes them constituent parts of the national sovereignty...and leaves in their possession certain exclusive and very important portions of sovereign power. This fully corresponds, in every rational import of the terms, with the idea of a Federal Government.

Alexander Hamilton (1787)

■ explain how and why the United States Constitution provides that laws of the national government and treaties are the supreme law of the land

■ explain how the distribution and sharing of power between the national and state governments increases opportunities for citizens to participate and to hold their governments accountable

B. What does the national government do?

The domestic and foreign policies established by the national government have significant consequences for the daily lives of all Americans.

Content summary and rationale

The actions of the national government have significant consequences on the daily lives of all Americans, their communities, and the welfare of the nation as a whole. These actions affect their security, their standard of living, and the taxes they will pay.

To understand the impact of the political process on their daily lives and the lives of their communities, citizens need to understand how the national government functions. To deliberate with other citizens about political action and to influence governmental actions that affect their lives, citizens need to know the allocation of responsibilities among various components of government and where and how decisions are made.

Content standards

1. **Major responsibilities for domestic and foreign policy.** *Students should be able to explain the major responsibilities of the national government for domestic and foreign policy.*

   To achieve this standard, students should be able to

   ■ identify historical and contemporary examples of important domestic policies, e.g., Pure Food and Drug Act, Environmental Protection Act, civil rights laws, child labor laws, minimum wage laws, Aid to Families with Dependent Children, Social Security

   ■ explain how and why domestic policies affect their lives

   ■ identify historical and contemporary examples of important foreign policies, e.g., Monroe Doctrine, Marshall Plan, immigration acts, foreign aid, arms control, promoting democracy and human rights throughout the world

   ■ explain how and why foreign policies affect own lives

Taxes are what we pay for civilized society.
Oliver Wendell Holmes, Jr.
(1904)

2. **Financing government through taxation.** *Students should be able to explain the necessity of taxes and the purposes for which taxes are used.*

   To achieve this standard, students should be able to

   ■ explain why taxation is necessary to pay for government

   ■ identify provisions of the United States Constitution that authorize the national government to collect taxes, i.e., Article One, Sections 7 and 8; Sixteenth Amendment

- identify major sources of revenue for the national government, e.g., individual income taxes, social insurance receipts (Social Security and Medicare), borrowing, taxes on corporations and businesses, estate and excise taxes, tariffs on foreign goods

- identify major uses of tax revenues received by the national government, e.g., direct payment to individuals (Social Security, Medicaid, Medicare, Aid to Families with Dependent Children), national defense, interest on the federal debt, interstate highways

C. How are state and local governments organized and what do they do?

Content summary and rationale

State governments are established by state constitutions. That is, each has its own legislative, executive, and judicial branches. States possess substantial powers that, along with their local and intermediate governments, affect a citizen's life from birth to death.

Local governments provide most of the services citizens receive, and local courts handle most civil disputes and violations of the law. State and local governments license businesses, professions, automobiles, and drivers; provide essential services such as police and fire protection, education, and street maintenance; regulate zoning and the construction of buildings; provide public housing, transportation, and public health services; and maintain streets, highways, airports, and harbors.

Because of their geographic location and the fact that their meetings usually are open to the public, state and local governments are often quite accessible to the people. Members of city councils, boards of education, mayors, governors, and other officials are often available to meet with individuals and groups and to speak to students and civic organizations.

Citizens need to know the purposes, organization, and responsibilities of their state and local governments so they can take part in their governance.

Local governments provide most of the services citizens receive.

Content standards

1. **State governments.** *Students should be able to explain why states have constitutions, their purposes, and the relationship of state constitutions to the federal constitution.*

   To achieve this standard, students should be able to

   - explain that their state has a constitution because the United States is a federal system

   - identify major purposes of the constitution of the state in which they live

   - identify and explain the basic similarities and differences between their state constitution and the United States Constitution

   - explain why state constitutions and state governments cannot violate the United States Constitution

   - explain how citizens can change their state constitution and cite examples of changes

2. Organization and responsibilities of state and local governments. *Students should be able to describe the organization and major responsibilities of state and local governments.*

To achieve this standard, students should be able to

- identify major responsibilities of their state and local governments, e.g., education, welfare, streets and roads, parks, recreation, and law enforcement

- describe the organization of their state and local governments, e.g., legislative, executive, and judicial functions at state and local levels

- identify major sources of revenue for state and local governments, e.g., property, sales, and income taxes; fees and licenses; taxes on corporations and businesses; borrowing

- explain why state and local governments have an important effect on their own lives

The support of State governments in all their rights, as the most competent administration of our domestic concerns, are the surest bulwarks against anti-republican tendencies.
Thomas Jefferson (1801)

D. Who represents you in local, state, and national governments?

Content summary and rationale

Few Americans can identify most of the key people elected to serve them. It is important not only to know who these people are, but what their responsibilities are, and how they can be contacted on matters of interest. Such knowledge is an essential first step in providing Americans with the capacity to take part in their own governance.

Content standards

1. Who represents you in legislative and executive branches of your local, state, and national governments? *Students should be able to identify their representatives in the legislative branches as well as the heads of the executive branches of their local, state, and national governments.*

To achieve this standard, students should be able to

- name the persons representing them at state and national levels in the legislative branches of government, i.e., representatives and senators in their state legislature and in Congress

- name the persons representing them at local, state, and national levels in the executive branches of government, e.g., mayor, governor, president

- explain how they can contact their representatives and when and why it is important to do so

- explain which level of government they should contact to express their opinions or to get help on specific problems, e.g., **opinions** about a curfew for persons under 16 years of age, an increase in state sales tax, aid to another country; **problems** with street lights, driver's license, federal income taxes

Few Americans can identify most of the key people elected to serve them.

E. What is the place of law in the American constitutional system?

Content summary and rationale

The rule of law operates within a framework provided by the United States Constitution. It establishes limits on both those who govern and the governed, making possible a system of ordered liberty which protects the basic rights of citizens and promotes the common good.

Law pervades American society. Americans look to the principal varieties of law—constitutional, civil, and criminal—for the protection of their rights to life, liberty, and property. It often is argued, however, that Americans are overly dependent on the legal system to manage disputes about social, economic, and political problems rather than using other means available to them such as private negotiations and participation in the political process.

An understanding of the place of law in the American constitutional system enhances citizens' capacity to

- appreciate the importance of law in protecting rights
- understand the importance of voluntary adherence to the law
- identify the purposes of American public life best served by law and the purposes best served by other means
- support new laws and changes in existing law that are in accord with the fundamental values and principles of the Constitution and serve the needs of their communities and the nation
- evaluate the operation of the legal system and proposals for improvement

Content standards

1. **The place of law in American society.** *Students should be able to explain the importance of law in the American constitutional system.*

To achieve this standard, students should be able to

- explain the importance of the rule of law in
  - establishing limits on both those who govern and the governed
  - protecting individual rights
  - promoting the common good
- describe historical and contemporary examples of the rule of law, e.g., *Marbury v. Madison, Brown v. Board of Education, U.S. v. Nixon*
- identify principal varieties of law, e.g., constitutional, criminal, civil
- explain how the principal varieties of law protect individual rights and promote the common good

Americans look to the principal varieties of law—constitutional, civil, and criminal—for the protection of their rights to life, liberty, and property.

If individuals enter into a state of society the laws of that society must be the supreme regulator of their conduct.

Alexander Hamilton (1788)

2. **Criteria for evaluating rules and laws.** *Students should be able to explain and apply criteria useful in evaluating rules and laws.*

    To achieve this standard, students should be able to

    ■ identify the strengths and weaknesses of a rule or law by determining if it is

    　■ well designed to achieve its purposes

    　■ understandable, i.e., clearly written, its requirements are explicit

    　■ possible to follow, i.e, does not demand the impossible

    　■ fair, i.e., not biased against or for any individual or group

    　■ designed to protect individual rights and to promote the common good

    ■ draft rules for their schools or communities that meet the criteria for a good or well-constructed rule or law

3. **Judicial protection of the rights of individuals.** *Students should be able to evaluate, take, and defend positions on current issues regarding judicial protection of individual rights.*

    To achieve this standard, students should be able to

    ■ explain the basic concept of due process of law, i.e., government must use fair procedures to gather information and make decisions in order to protect the rights of individuals and the interests of society

    ■ explain the importance to individuals and to society of major due process protections

    　■ habeas corpus

    　■ presumption of innocence

    　■ fair notice

    　■ impartial tribunal

    　■ speedy and public trials

    　■ right to counsel

    　■ trial by jury

    　■ right against self-incrimination

    　■ protection against double jeopardy

    　■ right of appeal

    ■ explain why due process rights in administrative and legislative procedures are essential for the protection of individual rights and the maintenance of limited government, e.g., the right to adequate notice of a hearing that may affect one's interests, the right to counsel in legislative hearings

    ■ describe the adversary system and evaluate its advantages and disadvantages

    ■ explain the basic principles of the juvenile justice system and the major differences between the due process rights of juveniles and adults

> *[N]or shall any State deprive any person of life, liberty, or property, without due process of law; nor deny to any person within its jurisdiction the equal protection of the laws.*
> **Fourteenth Amendment (1868)**

Center for Civic Education

■ describe alternative means of conflict management and evaluate their advantages and disadvantages, e.g., negotiation, mediation, arbitration, and litigation

■ evaluate arguments about current issues regarding judicial protection of the rights of individuals

F. How does the American political system provide for choice and opportunities for participation?

Content summary and rationale

The American political system provides citizens with numerous opportunities for choice and participation. The formal institutions and processes of government such as political parties, campaigns, and elections are important avenues for choice and citizen participation. Another equally important avenue is the many associations and groups that constitute civil society. All provide ways for citizens to monitor and influence the political process.

American constitutional democracy is dynamic and sometimes disorderly. Politics is not always smooth and predictable. Individually and in groups, citizens attempt to influence those in power. In turn, those in power attempt to influence citizens. In this process, the public agenda—the most pressing issues of the day—is set, and public opinion regarding these issues is formed.

If citizens do not understand the political process and how to deal with it effectively, they may feel overwhelmed and alienated. An understanding of the political process is a necessary prerequisite for effective and responsible participation in the making of public policy.

The American political system provides citizens with numerous opportunities for choice and participation.

Content standards

1. **The public agenda.** *Students should be able to explain what is meant by the public agenda and how it is set.*

    To achieve this standard, students should be able to

    ■ explain that the public agenda consists of those matters that occupy public attention at any particular time, e.g., crime, health care, education, child care, environmental protection, drug abuse

    ■ describe how the public agenda is shaped by political leaders, interest groups, the media, state and federal courts, individual citizens

    ■ explain how individuals can help to shape the public agenda, e.g., by joining interest groups or political parties, by making presentations at public meetings, by writing letters to government officials and to newspapers

2. **Political communication.** *Students should be able to evaluate, take, and defend positions on the influence of the media on American political life.*

To achieve this standard, students should be able to

- explain the importance of freedom of the press to informed participation in the political system

- evaluate the influence of television, radio, the press, newsletters, and emerging means of electronic communication on American politics

- explain how Congress, the president, the Supreme Court, and state and local public officials use the media to communicate with the citizenry

- explain how citizens can evaluate information and arguments received from various sources so that they can make reasonable choices on public issues and among candidates for political office

- evaluate opportunities the media provide for individuals to monitor actions of their government, e.g., televised broadcasts of proceedings of governmental agencies, such as Congress and the courts, press conferences held by public officials

- evaluate opportunities the media provide for individuals to communicate their concerns and positions on current issues, e.g., letters to the editor, talk shows, "op-ed pages," public opinion polls

3. **Political parties, campaigns, and elections.** *Students should be able to explain how political parties, campaigns, and elections provide opportunities for citizens to participate in the political process.*

To achieve this standard, students should be able to

- describe the role of political parties

- describe various kinds of elections, e.g., primary and general, local and state, congressional, presidential, recall

- explain ways individuals can participate in political parties, campaigns, and elections

4. **Associations and groups.** *Students should be able to explain how interest groups, unions, and professional organizations provide opportunities for citizens to participate in the political process.*

To achieve this standard, students should be able to

- describe the historical roles of prominent associations and groups in local, state, or national politics, e.g., abolitionists, suffragists, labor unions, agricultural organizations, civil rights groups, religious organizations

- describe the contemporary roles of prominent associations and groups in local, state, or national politics, e.g., AFL-CIO, National Education Association, Chamber of Commerce, Common Cause, League of Women Voters, American Medical Association, National Rifle Association, Greenpeace, National Association for the Advancement of Colored People (NAACP), Public Citizen, World Wildlife Federation

I fear three newspapers more than a hundred bayonets.
Napoleon Bonaparte (c.1800)

Better use has been made of association and this powerful instrument of action has been applied for more varied aims in America than anywhere else in the world.
Alexis de Tocqueville (1835)

Center for Civic Education

- explain how and why Americans become members of associations and groups

- explain how individuals can participate in the political process through membership in associations and groups

5. **Forming and carrying out public policy.** *Students should be able to explain how public policy is formed and carried out at local, state, and national levels and what roles individuals can play in the process.*

   To achieve this standard, students should be able to

   - define public policy and identify examples at local, state, and national levels

   - describe how public policies are formed and implemented

   - explain how citizens can monitor and influence the formation and implementation of public policies

   - explain why conflicts about values, principles, and interests may make agreement difficult or impossible on certain issues of public policy, e.g., affirmative action, gun control, environmental protection, capital punishment, equal rights

IV. WHAT IS THE RELATIONSHIP OF THE UNITED STATES TO OTHER NATIONS AND TO WORLD AFFAIRS?

A. How is the world organized politically?

Content summary and rationale

The world is divided into **nation-states** each of which claims sovereignty over a defined territory and jurisdiction over everyone within it. These nation-states interact using diplomacy, formal agreements, and sanctions, which may be peaceful or may involve the use of force.

At the international level there is no political organization with power comparable to that of the nation-state to make binding decisions and enforce agreements. As a result, when conflicts arise among nation-states, wars may erupt on local, regional, or worldwide levels.

There are, however, governmental and nongovernmental international organizations that provide avenues through which nation-states can interact and attempt to manage their affairs and conflicts peacefully.

To make judgments about the role of the United States in the world today and the course American foreign policy should take, citizens need to understand some of the major elements of international relations and how world affairs affect them.

The world is divided into nation-states each of which claims sovereignty over a defined territory and jurisdiction over everyone within it.

Content standards

1. **Nation-states.** *Students should be able to explain how the world is organized politically.*

    To achieve this standard, students should be able to

    - describe how the world is divided into nation-states that claim sovereignty over a defined territory and jurisdiction over everyone within it

    - explain why there is no political organization at the international level with power comparable to that of the nation-state

2. **Interaction among nation-states.** *Students should be able to explain how nation-states interact with each other.*

    To achieve this standard, students should be able to

    - describe the most important means nation-states use to interact with one another
        - trade
        - diplomacy
        - treaties and agreements
        - humanitarian aid
        - economic incentives and sanctions
        - military force and the threat of force

If we do not want to die together in war, we must learn to live together in peace.
Harry S. Truman (1945)

■ explain reasons for the breakdown of order among nation-states, e.g, conflicts about national interests, ethnicity, and religion; competition for resources and territory; absence of effective means to enforce international law

■ explain the consequences of the breakdown of order among nation-states

■ explain why and how the breakdown of order among nation-states can affect their own lives

3. **United States' relations with other nation-states.** *Students should be able to explain how United States foreign policy is made and the means by which it is carried out.*

To achieve this standard, students should be able to

■ explain the most important powers the United States Constitution gives to the Congress, president, and federal judiciary in foreign affairs

   ■ Congress—can declare war, approve treaties (Senate), raise and support armies, and provide a navy (Article I, Section 8)

   ■ president—is Commander in Chief, can make treaties and appoint ambassadors (Article II)

   ■ federal judiciary—can decide cases affecting treaties and ambassadors, and those involving treason (Article III)

■ describe various means used to attain the ends of United States foreign policy, e.g., diplomacy; economic, military, and humanitarian aid; treaties; trade agreements; incentives; sanctions; military intervention; covert action

■ identify important current foreign policy issues and evaluate the means the United States is using to deal with them

4. **International organizations.** *Students should be able to explain the role of major international organizations in the world today.*

To achieve this standard, students should be able to

■ describe the purposes and functions of major governmental international organizations, e.g., UN, NATO, OAS, World Court

■ describe the purposes and functions of major nongovernmental international organizations, e.g., International Red Cross, World Council of Churches, Amnesty International

B. How has the United States influenced other nations and how have other nations influenced American politics and society?

Content summary and rationale

The United States does not exist in isolation; it is part of an interconnected world in whose development it has played and continues to play an important role. The American political tradition, including the ideas expressed in the Declaration of Independence, the Constitution, and the Bill of Rights, has had a profound influence abroad. In turn,

Americans have been affected by the political ideas of other nations from the ideas of the natural rights philosophers and classical republicanism of the founding period to ideas about social and economic rights such as those found in the Universal Declaration of Human Rights.

Political, economic, demographic, and environmental developments in the world affect Americans and require the United States to respond with reasoned and effective policies to deal with them. Because of the interconnectedness of the world, many pressing domestic problems, including the economy and the environment, are also international issues. Thus, what once was considered a clear distinction between domestic and international policy is no longer valid in some cases.

To take part in debate about domestic and foreign policy, citizens need to be aware of developments in the world and their effects, and to evaluate proposals for dealing with them.

Content standards

1. **Impact of the American concept of democracy and individual rights on the world.** *Students should be able to describe the influence of American political ideas on other nations.*

   To achieve this standard, students should be able to

   ■ describe the impact on other nations of the American Revolution and of the values and principles expressed in the Declaration of Independence and the United States Constitution, including the Bill of Rights

   ■ describe the influence American ideas about rights have had on other nations and international organizations, e.g., French Revolution; democracy movements in Eastern Europe, People's Republic of China, Latin America, South Africa; United Nations Charter; Universal Declaration of Human Rights

   ■ describe the impact of other nations' ideas about rights on the United States, e.g., natural rights in the seventeenth and eighteenth centuries, social and economic rights in the twentieth century

2. **Political, demographic, and environmental developments.** *Students should be able to explain the effects of significant political, demographic, and environmental trends in the world.*

   To achieve this standard, students should be able to

   ■ describe the impact of current political developments in the world on the United States, e.g., conflicts within and among other nations, efforts to establish democratic governments

   ■ describe the impact of major demographic trends on the United States, e.g., population growth, increase in immigration and refugees

   ■ describe environmental conditions that affect the United States, e.g., destruction of rain forests and animal habitats, depletion of fishing grounds, air and water pollution

Just what is it that America stands for? If she stands for one thing more than another, it is for the sovereignty of self-governing people....She stands as an example of free institutions, and as an example of disinterested international action in the main tenets of justice.
Woodrow Wilson (1916)

[T]he Declaration of Independence...gave liberty not alone to the people of this country, but hope to all the world, for all future time.
Abraham Lincoln (1861)

V. WHAT ARE THE ROLES OF THE CITIZEN IN AMERICAN DEMOCRACY?

A. What is citizenship?

Content summary and rationale

Citizenship in a constitutional democracy differs from membership in an authoritarian or totalitarian regime. In a democracy each citizen is a full and equal member of a self-governing community endowed with fundamental rights and entrusted with responsibilities.

Both the government and the citizens of a constitutional democracy are responsible for the protection of the rights of individuals and for the promotion of the common good. It is a fundamental responsibility of the citizen to see that government serves the purposes for which it was created.

In order to fulfill this role, individuals need to understand what citizenship in a constitutional democracy means.

Content standards

1. **The meaning of citizenship.** *Students should be able to explain the meaning of American citizenship.*

   To achieve this standard, students should be able to

   - explain the important characteristics of citizenship in the United States. Specifically, citizenship

     - is legally recognized membership in a self-governing community

     - confers full membership in a self-governing community—there are no degrees of citizenship or of legally tolerated states of inferior citizenship in the United States

     - confers equal rights under the law

     - is not dependent on inherited, involuntary groupings such as race, gender, or ethnicity

     - confers certain rights and privileges, e.g., the right to vote, to hold public office, to serve on juries

   - explain that Americans are citizens of both their state and the United States

2. **Becoming a citizen.** Students should be able to explain how one becomes a citizen of the United States.

   To achieve this standard, students should be able to

   - explain that anyone born in the United States is a U.S. citizen

   - explain the distinction between citizens and noncitizens (aliens)

   - describe the process by which noncitizens may become citizens

   - compare naturalization in the United States with that of other nations

In view of the Constitution, in the eye of the law, there is in this country no superior, dominant, ruling class of citizens. There is no caste here. Our Constitution is color-blind, and neither knows nor tolerates classes among citizens. In respect of civil rights, all citizens are equal before the law. The humblest is the peer of the most powerful.
John Marshall Harlan (1896)

Center for Civic Education

- evaluate the criteria established by law that are used for admission to citizenship in the United States

    - residence in the United States for five years

    - ability to read, write, and speak English

    - proof of good moral character

    - knowledge of the history of the United States

    - knowledge of and support for the values and principles of American constitutional democracy

B. What are the rights of citizens?

Content summary and rationale

In a political system in which one of the primary purposes of government is the protection of individual rights, it is important for citizens to understand what these rights are and their relationship to each other and to other values and interests of their society.

The concept of rights is complex and cannot be treated thoroughly in these standards. These standards, however, will provide a basis for the analysis of public issues involving rights. It is useful to distinguish among three categories of rights that are of particular significance in the American political system. These are the right to a private or personal domain, political, and economic rights.

Few rights, if any, are considered absolute. Rights may reinforce or conflict with each other or with other values and interests necessitating reasonable limitations on them. It is important, therefore, for citizens to develop a framework that clarifies their ideas about rights and the relationships among rights and other values and interests. Such a framework provides citizens with a basis for making reasoned decisions about the proper scope and limits of rights.

The right of the people to be secure in their persons, houses, papers, and effects, against unreasonable searches and seizures, shall not be violated....

Fourth Amendment (1791)

Content standards

1. **Personal rights.** *Students should be able to evaluate, take, and defend positions on issues involving personal rights.*

    To achieve this standard, students should be able to

    - identify personal rights, e.g., freedom of conscience, freedom to marry whom one chooses, to have children, to associate with whomever one pleases, to live where one chooses, to travel freely, to emigrate

    - identify the major documentary sources of personal rights, e.g., Declaration of Independence, United States Constitution, including the Bill of Rights, state constitutions

    - explain the importance to the individual and to society of such personal rights as

        - freedom of conscience and religion

        - freedom of expression and association

        - freedom of movement and residence

        - privacy

■ identify and evaluate contemporary issues that involve personal rights, e.g., restricting membership in private organizations, school prayer, dress codes, curfews, sexual harassment, the right to refuse medical care

Congress shall make no law respecting an establishment of religion, or prohibiting the free exercise thereof; or abridging the freedom of speech, or of the press; or the right of the people peaceably to assemble, and to petition the Government for a redress of grievances.

First Amendment (1791)

2. **Political rights.** *Students should be able to evaluate, take, and defend positions on issues involving political rights.*

To achieve this standard, students should be able to

■ identify political rights, e.g., the right to vote, petition, assembly, freedom of press

■ explain the meaning of political rights as distinguished from personal rights, e.g., the right of free speech for political discussion as distinct from the right of free speech to express personal tastes and interests, the right to register to vote as distinct from the right to live where one chooses

■ identify major statements of political rights in documents such as the Declaration of Independence, United States Constitution, including the Bill of Rights, state constitutions, and civil rights legislation

■ explain the importance to the individual and society of such political rights as

■ freedom of speech, press, assembly, and petition

■ right to vote and to seek public office

■ identify and evaluate contemporary issues that involve political rights, e.g., hate speech, fair trial, free press

3. **Economic rights.** *Students should be able to evaluate, take, and defend positions on issues involving economic rights.*

To achieve this standard, students should be able to

■ identify important economic rights, e.g., the right to own property, choose one's work, change employment, join a labor union, establish a business

■ identify statements of economic rights in the United States Constitution, e.g., requirement of just compensation, contracts, copyright, patents

■ explain the importance to the individual and to society of such economic rights as the right to

■ acquire, use, transfer, and dispose of property

■ choose one's work, change employment

■ join labor unions and professional associations

■ establish and operate a business

■ copyright and patent

■ enter into lawful contracts

As a jury trial is drawn from the primary right to a fair trial... so earning is implicit in equal American citizenship.

Judith Shklar (1991)

■ identify and evaluate contemporary issues regarding economic rights, e.g., employment, welfare, social security, minimum wage, health care, equal pay for equal work, freedom of contract

4. **Scope and limits of rights.** *Students should be able to evaluate, take, and defend positions on issues regarding the proper scope and limits of rights.*

To achieve this standard, students should be able to

- explain what is meant by the "scope and limits" of a right, e.g., the scope of one's right to free speech in the United States is extensive and protects almost all forms of political expression. The right to free speech, however, can be limited if and when that speech seriously harms or endangers others

- explain the argument that all rights have limits

- explain criteria commonly used in determining what limits should be placed on specific rights, e.g.,

    - clear and present danger rule
    - compelling government interest test
    - national security
    - libel or slander
    - public safety
    - equal opportunity

- identify and evaluate positions on a contemporary conflict between rights, e.g., right to a fair trial and right to a free press, right to privacy and right to freedom of expression

- identify and evaluate positions on a contemporary conflict between rights and other social values and interests, e.g., the right of the public to know what their government is doing versus the need for national security, the right to property versus the protection of the environment

C. What are the responsibilities of citizens?

Content summary and rationale

An examination of the importance of personal and political and economic rights must be accompanied by an examination of personal and civic responsibilities. For American constitutional democracy to flourish and seek to attain its ideals, citizens must not only be aware of their rights, they must also exercise them responsibly and fulfill those personal and civic responsibilities necessary in a self-governing, free, and just society.

Citizens must examine the basic values and principles of the United States Constitution and monitor the performance of political leaders and government agencies to insure their fidelity to them. In addition, they must examine their own behavior in relation to those values and principles and learn to deal appropriately with situations in which their responsibilities may require that their personal rights, desires, or interests be subordinated to the common good.

To make judgments about their responsibilities, citizens must understand the difference between personal and civic responsibilities as well as the mutual reinforcement of these responsibilities.

The most stringent protection of free speech would not protect a man in falsely shouting fire in a theater and causing a panic.

Oliver Wendell Holmes, Jr.
(1919)

In Germany the Nazis came first for the Communists, and I didn't speak up because I wasn't a Communist. Then they came for the Jews, and I didn't speak up because I wasn't a Jew. Then they came for the trade unionists, and I didn't speak up because I wasn't a trade unionist. Then they came for the Catholics, and I didn't speak up because I was a Protestant. Then they came for me, and by that time no one was left to speak up.

Attributed to Martin Niemoeller
(c.1949)

As citizens of this democracy, you are the rulers and the ruled, the lawgivers and the law-abiding, the beginning and the end.

Adlai Stevenson (c.1956)

Content standards

1. **Personal responsibilities.** *Students should be able to evaluate, take, and defend positions on the importance of personal responsibilities to the individual and to society.*

   To achieve this standard, students should be able to

   - evaluate the importance of commonly held personal responsibilities, such as
     - taking care of one's self
     - supporting one's family
     - accepting responsibility for the consequences of one's actions
     - adhering to moral principles
     - considering the rights and interests of others
     - behaving in a civil manner
   - identify and evaluate contemporary issues that involve personal responsibilities, e.g., failure to provide adequate support or care for one's children, cheating on examinations, lack of concern for the less fortunate

2. **Civic responsibilities.** *Students should be able to evaluate, take, and defend positions on the importance of civic responsibilities to the individual and society.*

   To achieve this standard, students should be able to

   - evaluate the importance of commonly held civic responsibilities, such as
     - obeying the law
     - paying taxes
     - respecting the rights of others
     - being informed and attentive to public issues
     - monitoring political leaders and governmental agencies and taking appropriate action if their adherence to constitutional principles is lacking
     - deciding whether and how to vote
     - participating in civic groups
     - performing public service
     - serving as a juror
     - serving in the armed forces
   - explain the meaning of civic responsibilities as distinguished from personal responsibilities
   - evaluate when their responsibilities as Americans require that their personal rights and interests be subordinated to the public good
   - evaluate the importance for the individual and society of fulfilling civic responsibilities
   - identify and evaluate contemporary issues that involve civic responsibilities, e.g., low voter participation, avoidance of jury duty, failure to be informed about public issues

D. What dispositions or traits of character are important to the preservation and improvement of American constitutional democracy?

Content summary and rationale

American constitutional democracy requires the responsible self-governance of each individual. Certain traits of private character such as moral responsibility, self-discipline, and respect for individual worth and human dignity are essential to the well-being of the society.

No democracy can accomplish its purposes, however, unless its citizens are inclined to participate thoughtfully in public affairs. Certain traits of public character such as civility, respect for law, civic mindedness, critical mindedness, persistence, and a willingness to negotiate and compromise are indispensable for the vitality of American constitutional democracy.

Such traits of private and public character also contribute to the fulfillment of the individual and to his or her efficacy as a citizen.

Content standards

1. **Dispositions that enhance citizen effectiveness and promote the healthy functioning of American constitutional democracy.** *Students should be able to evaluate, take, and defend positions on the importance of certain dispositions or traits of character to themselves and American constitutional democracy.*

   To achieve this standard, students should be able to

   - explain the importance to the individual and society of the following dispositions or traits of character

     - **individual responsibility**—fulfilling the moral and legal obligations of membership in society

     - **self-discipline/self-governance**—adhering voluntarily to self-imposed standards of behavior rather than requiring the imposition of external controls

     - **civility**—treating other persons respectfully, regardless of whether or not one agrees with their viewpoints; being willing to listen to other points of view; avoiding hostile, abusive, emotional, and illogical argument

     - **courage**—the strength to stand up for one's convictions when conscience demands

     - **respect for the rights of other individuals**—having respect for others' right to an equal voice in government, to be equal in the eyes of the law, to hold and advocate diverse ideas, and to join in associations to advance their views

     - **respect for law**—willingness to abide by laws, even though one may not be in complete agreement with every law; willingness to work through peaceful, legal means to change laws which are thought to be unwise or unjust

     - **honesty**—willingness to seek and express the truth

     - **open mindedness**—considering others' points of view

I often wonder whether we do not rest our hopes too much upon constitutions, upon laws and upon courts. These are false hopes; believe me, these are false hopes. Liberty lies in the hearts of men and women; when it dies there, no constitution, no law, no court can save it....
Learned Hand (1941, 1944)

Civility costs nothing and buys everything.
Lady Mary Wortley Montagu
(1756)

[A purpose of government is] to inbreed and cherish in a great people the seeds of virtu, *and public civility*
John Milton (1641)

Center for Civic Education

- **critical mindedness**—having the inclination to question the validity of various positions, including one's own

- **negotiation and compromise**—making an effort to come to agreement with those with whom one may differ, when it is reasonable and morally justifiable to do so

- **persistence**—being willing to attempt again and again to accomplish worthwhile goals

- **civic mindedness**—paying attention to and having concern for public affairs

- **compassion**—having concern for the well-being of others, especially for the less fortunate

- **patriotism**—being loyal to the values and principles underlying American constitutional democracy, as distinguished from jingoism and chauvinism

E. How can citizens take part in civic life?

Content summary and rationale

The well-being of constitutional democracy depends on the informed and effective participation of citizens concerned with the preservation of individual rights and the promotion of the common good. The strength and significance of Americans' participatory habits were remarked upon in the nineteenth century by Alexis de Tocqueville, who was struck by the degree of their social participation. Americans have retained this characteristic of engaging in cooperative action for common purposes. Participation in government, contrasted with the wider realm of organized social participation, has ebbed in recent decades, however. Indifference to or alienation from politics characterizes a significant segment of the population. Citizens should realize that their intelligence and energy are needed in political forums and that democracy wanes when citizens shun politics.

There are two general ways to approach problems that confront society. One is through **social action**; the other is through **political action**. For example, in dealing with crime, a course of social action might include forming a neighborhood watch. A course of political action might include meeting with officials and demanding that police provide adequate protection. In dealing with hunger, social action might include working in a soup kitchen organized by a charitable organization; political action might include devising a government program to feed the hungry and acting to insure its adoption and public funding.

Social and political action are not mutually exclusive; they may overlap. At times, one approach may be more appropriate or desirable than another. Nevertheless, both political and social action are essential for the health of American constitutional democracy.

If citizens want their views to be considered, they must become active participants in the political process. Although elections, campaigns, and voting are at the center of democratic institutions, citizens should be aware that beyond electoral politics there is a wide range of participatory opportunities available to them. These possibilities include attending political meetings, contacting public officials, joining advocacy groups and political parties, and taking part in demonstrations.

Political leadership and careers in public service are vitally important in American constitutional democracy. Citizens need to understand the contributions of those in public service as well as the practical and ethical dilemmas political leaders face.

To answer the question "Why should I participate in the political system?" the citizen needs to examine and evaluate the relationship between the attainment of individual and public goals and participation in the civic and political life of the community.

If American constitutional democracy is to endure, its citizens must recognize that it is not "a machine that would go of itself." They also must be aware of the difficulty of establishing free institutions, as evidenced by the experience of the Founders as well as by events in the contemporary world. Constitutional democracy requires the continuing and dedicated participation of an attentive, knowledgeable, and reflective citizenry.

Whether in private or in public, the good citizen does something to support democratic habits and the constitutional order.
Judith Shklar (1991)

Content standards

1. **Participation in civic and political life and the attainment of individual and public goals.** *Students should be able to explain the relationship between participating in civic and political life and the attainment of individual and public goals.*

   To achieve this standard, students should be able to

   - identify examples of their own individual goals and explain how their participation in civic and political life can help to attain them, e.g., living in a safe and orderly neighborhood, obtaining a good education, living in a healthy environment

   - identify examples of public goals and explain how participation in civic and political life can help to attain them, e.g., increasing the safety of the community, improving local transportation facilities, providing opportunities for education and recreation

2. **The difference between political and social participation.** *Students should be able to explain the difference between political and social participation.*

   To achieve this standard, students should be able to

   - explain what distinguishes political from social participation, e.g., participating in a campaign to change laws regulating the care of children as opposed to volunteering to care for children

   - explain the importance of both political and social participation to American constitutional democracy

   - identify opportunities in their own community for both political and social participation

Where everyman is...participator in the government of affairs, not merely at an election one day in the year but every day...he will let the heart be torn out of his body sooner than his power be wrested from him by a Caesar or a Bonaparte.
Thomas Jefferson (1816)

I contend that woman has just as much right to sit in solemn counsel in conventions, conferences, associations and general assemblies, as man—just as much right to sit upon the throne of England or in the Presidential chair of the United States.

Angelina Grimke (1837)

[A]mong free men, there can be no successful appeal from the ballot to the bullet; and...they who take such appeal are sure to lose their case, and pay the cost.

Abraham Lincoln (1863)

The aim of every political constitution is, or ought to be, first to obtain for rulers men who possess most wisdom to discern and most virtue to pursue, the common good of the society and in the next place, to take the most effectual precaution for keeping them virtuous whilst they continue to hold their public trust.

James Madison (1787)

3. **Forms of political participation.** *Students should be able to describe the means by which Americans can monitor and influence politics and government.*

To achieve this standard, students should be able to

■ explain how Americans can use the following means to monitor and influence politics and government at local, state, and national levels

  ■ voting

  ■ becoming informed about public issues

  ■ discussing public issues

  ■ communicating with public officials

  ■ joining political parties, interest groups, and other organizations that attempt to influence public policy and elections

  ■ attending meetings of governing bodies

  ■ working in campaigns

  ■ taking part in peaceful demonstration

  ■ circulating and signing petitions

  ■ contributing money to political parties or causes

■ describe historical and current examples of citizen movements seeking to promote individual rights and the common good, e.g., abolition, suffrage, labor and civil rights movements

■ explain what civil disobedience is, how it differs from other forms of protest, what its consequences might be, and circumstances under which it might be justified

■ explain why becoming knowledgeable about public affairs and the values and principles of American constitutional democracy and communicating that knowledge to others is a form of political participation

4. **Political leadership and public service.** *Students should be able to explain the importance of political leadership and public service in a constitutional democracy.*

To achieve this standard, students should be able to

■ describe personal qualities necessary for political leadership

■ explain the functions of political leadership and why leadership is a vital necessity in a constitutional democracy

■ explain and evaluate ethical dilemmas that might confront political leaders

■ identify opportunities for political leadership in their own school, community, state, and the nation

■ explain the importance of individuals working cooperatively with their elected leaders

■ evaluate the role of "the loyal opposition" in a constitutional democracy

- explain the importance of public service in a constitutional democracy
- identify opportunities for public service in their own school, community, state and the nation
- identify career opportunities in public service

5. **Knowledge and participation**. *Students should be able to explain the importance of knowledge to competent and responsible participation in American democracy.*

To achieve this standard, students should be able to

- explain why becoming knowledgeable about public affairs and the values and principles of American constitutional democracy and communicating that knowledge to others is an important form of participation
- explain how awareness of the nature of American constitutional democracy may give citizens the ability to reaffirm or change fundamental constitutional values
- evaluate the claim that constitutional democracy requires the participation of an attentive, knowledgeable, and competent citizenry

A leader has to lead, or otherwise he has no business in politics.
Harry Truman (c.1955)

If a nation expects to be ignorant and free, in a state of civilization, it expects what never was and never will be.
Thomas Jefferson (1816)

Center for Civic Education

9-12 Content Standards

9-12 Content Standards

I. WHAT ARE CIVIC LIFE, POLITICS, AND GOVERNMENT?

A. What is civic life? What is politics? What is government? Why are government and politics necessary? What purposes should government serve?

Content summary and rationale

Civic life is the public life of the citizen concerned with the affairs of the community and nation as contrasted with private or personal life, which is devoted to the pursuit of private and personal interests.

Politics is a process by which a group of people, whose opinions or interests might be divergent, reach collective decisions that are generally regarded as binding on the group and enforced as common policy. Political life enables people to accomplish goals they could not realize as individuals. Politics necessarily arises whenever groups of people live together, since they must always reach collective decisions of one kind or another.

Government is the formal institutions of a society with the authority to make and implement binding decisions about such matters as the distribution of resources, allocation of benefits and burdens, and the management of conflicts.

Differing assumptions about the proper relationship between civic and private life influence ideas about the purposes of government. Differing ideas about the purposes of government have profound consequences for the well-being of individuals and society. For example, if one believes that the activities of government should be restricted to providing for the security of the lives and property of citizens, one might believe in placing severe restrictions on the right of government to intrude into their private or personal lives. On the other hand, if one believes that the moral character of the individual should be a public or civic matter, one might support a broad range of laws and regulations concerning private behavior and belief.

Citizens need to understand competing ideas about civic life, politics, and government so that they can make informed judgments about what government should and should not do, how they are to live their lives together, and how to support the proper use of authority or combat the abuse of political power.

Politics is a process by which a group of people, whose opinions or interests might be divergent, reach collective decisions that are generally regarded as binding on the group and enforced as common policy.

Differing ideas about the purposes of government have profound consequences for the well-being of individuals and society.

Content standards

1. **Defining civic life, politics, and government**. *Students should be able to explain the meaning of the terms civic life, politics, and government.*

   To achieve this standard, students should be able to

   ■ distinguish between **civic life**—the public life of the citizen concerned with the affairs of the community and nation—and **private life**—the personal life of the individual devoted to the pursuit of private interests

- describe **politics** as the process by which a group of people, whose opinions or interests might be divergent,

  - reach collective decisions that are generally regarded as binding on the group and enforced as common policy

  - seek the power to influence decisions about such matters as how their government will manage the distribution of resources, allocation of benefits and burdens, and management of conflicts

  - accomplish goals they could not realize as individuals

- describe **government** as the formal institutions with the authority to make and implement binding decisions about such matters as the distribution of resources, the allocation of benefits and burdens, and the management of conflicts

  - define political authority, identify its sources and functions, and differentiate between authority and power without authority

  - identify examples of formal institutions with the authority to control and direct the behavior of those in a society, e.g., tribal councils, courts, monarchies, democratic legislatures

2. **Necessity of politics and government**. *Students should be able to explain the major arguments advanced for the necessity of politics and government.*

   To achieve this standard, students should be able to

   - explain why politics is found wherever people gather together, i.e., it is a process by which a group of people reach collective decisions generally regarded as binding on the group and enforced as common policy

   - explain several major arguments for the necessity of politics and government, e.g., because human beings

     - cannot fulfill their potential without politics and government

     - are sinful or depraved by nature

     - would be insecure or endangered without government

     - working collectively can accomplish goals and solve problems they could not achieve alone

   - describe historical and contemporary examples of how governments have reflected these major arguments

3. **The purposes of politics and government**. *Students should be able to evaluate, take, and defend positions on competing ideas regarding the purposes of politics and government and their implications for the individual and society.*

   To achieve this standard, students should be able to

   - explain competing ideas about the purposes of politics and government, e.g.,

     - improving the moral character of citizens

     - furthering the interests of a particular class or ethnic group

[Without government:] No arts; no letters; no society; and which is worst of all, continual fear and danger of violent death; and the life of man, solitary, poor, nasty, brutish, and short.

Thomas Hobbes (1651)

We hold these Truths to be self-evident, that all Men are created equal, that they are endowed by their Creator with certain unalienable Rights...That to secure these Rights, Governments are instituted among Men.

Declaration of Independence (1776)

- achieving a religious vision
- glorifying the state
- promoting individual security and public order
- enhancing economic prosperity
- protecting individual rights
- promoting the common good
- providing for a nation's security

■ describe historical and contemporary examples of governments which serve these purposes

■ explain how the purposes served by a government affect relationships between the individual and government and between government and society as a whole, e.g., the purpose of promoting a religious vision of what society should be like may require a government to restrict individual thought and actions and place strict controls on the whole of society

B. What are the essential characteristics of limited and unlimited government?

Content summary and rationale

Limited government provides a basis for protecting individual rights and promoting the common good in contrast to unlimited government which endangers these values. Limited government is constitutional government. Unlimited governments include authoritarian and totalitarian systems.

The **rule of law** is an essential component of limited government. The central notion of a rule of law is that society is governed according to widely known and accepted rules followed not only by the governed but also by those in authority.

Civil society is that sphere of voluntary individual, social, and economic relationships and organizations that, although limited by law, is not part of governmental institutions. Civil society provides a domain where individuals are free from unreasonable interference from government. By providing for independent centers of power and influence, civil society is an indispensable means of maintaining limited government.

Political and economic freedoms and limited government are interrelated. Limited government protects both political and economic freedoms which, in turn, provide a means of maintaining and reinforcing limited government.

An awareness of the characteristics of limited government provides citizens with a basis for making reasoned judgments about proposals to alter their own government and for evaluating the governments of other nations.

An understanding of the concept of limited government and its essential components helps citizens understand the necessity of maintaining those conditions that prevent a government from exceeding its powers.

[A purpose of government is] to inbreed and cherish in a great people the seeds of virtu, *and public civility.*
John Milton (1641)

In framing a government which is to be administered by men over men, the great difficulty lies in this: you must first enable the government to control the governed; and in the next place oblige it to control itself.
James Madison (1788)

Civil society is that sphere of voluntary individual, social, and economic relationships and organizations that, although limited by law, is not part of governmental institutions. Civil society provides a domain where individuals are free from unreasonable interference from government.

No freeman shall be taken, or imprisoned, or outlawed, or exiled, or in any way harmed...except by the legal judgment of his peers or by the law of the land.
Magna Carta (1215)

Power tends to corrupt and absolute power corrupts absolutely.
Lord Acton (1887)

Wherever Law ends, Tyranny begins.
John Locke (1690)

Content standards

1. **Limited and unlimited governments.** *Students should be able to explain the essential characteristics of limited and unlimited governments.*

To achieve this standard students should be able to

■ describe the essential characteristics of limited and unlimited governments

■ limited governments have established and respected restraints on their power, e.g.,

■ constitutional government—governments characterized by legal limits on political power

■ unlimited governments are those in which there are no regularized and effective means of restraining their power, i.e.,

■ authoritarian systems—governments in which political power is concentrated in one person or a small group, and individuals and groups are subordinated to that power

■ totalitarian systems—modern forms of extreme authoritarianism in which the government attempts to control every aspect of the lives of individuals and prohibits independent associations

■ identify historical and contemporary examples of limited and unlimited governments and explain their classification, e.g.,

■ limited governments—United States, Great Britain, Botswana, Japan, Israel, Chile

■ unlimited governments—Nazi Germany, Imperial Japan, Spain under Franco, Argentina under Peron, Iraq under Hussein, Iran

2. **The rule of law.** *Students should be able to evaluate, take, and defend positions on the importance of the rule of law and on the sources, purposes, and functions of law.*

To achieve this standard, students should be able to

■ explain the difference between the rule of law and the "rule of men"

■ explain why the rule of law means more than simply having laws

■ explain alternative ideas about the sources of law, e.g., custom, Supreme Being, sovereigns, legislatures

■ identify different varieties of law, e.g., divine law, natural law, common law, statute law, international law

■ explain alternative ideas about the purposes and functions of law such as

■ regulating relationships among people and between people and their government

■ providing order, predictability, security, and established procedures for the management of conflict

- specifying the allocation of rights and responsibilities and of benefits and burdens
- providing the ultimate source of authority in a political community
- regulating social and economic relationships in civil society
- explain how the rule of law can be used to restrict the actions of private citizens and government officials alike in order to protect the rights of individuals and to promote the common good

3. **Civil society and government.** *Students should be able to explain and evaluate the argument that civil society is a prerequisite of limited government.*

To achieve this standard, students should be able to

- define civil society as the sphere of voluntary personal, social, and economic relationships and organizations that, although limited by law, is not part of government, e.g., family, friendships, membership in nongovernmental organizations, participation in unions and business enterprises
- explain how civil society provides opportunities for individuals to associate for social, cultural, religious, economic, and political purposes
- explain how civil society makes it possible for people individually or in association with others to bring their influence to bear on government in ways other than voting and elections
- describe the historical role of religion in the development of a private sphere of life
- explain, using historical and contemporary examples, how the resources of civil society have been used to maintain limited government
- compare the relationships between government and civil society in constitutional democracies and in authoritarian and totalitarian regimes using historical and contemporary examples

Civil society makes it possible for people individually or in association with others to bring their influence to bear on government in ways other than voting and elections.

4. **The relationship of limited government to political and economic freedom.** *Students should be able to explain and evaluate competing ideas regarding the relationship between political and economic freedoms.*

To achieve this standard, students should be able to

- identify essential political freedoms, e.g., freedom of religion, speech, press, and assembly
- identify essential economic freedoms, e.g., freedom to enter into contracts, choose one's own employment, own and dispose of property, engage in business enterprises
- explain competing ideas about the relationship between political and economic freedoms, e.g., that political freedom is more important than economic freedom, that political and economic freedom are inseparable

Though written constitutions may be violated in moments of passion or delusion, yet they furnish a text to which those who are watchful may again rally and recall the people; they fix too for the people the principles of their political creed.

Thomas Jefferson (1802)

Articles 114, 115, 117, 118, 123, 124 and 153 of the constitution of the German Reich are cancelled until further notice. This allows certain restrictions to be imposed on personal freedom, on the right to express a free opinion, the freedom of the press, of association and the right to hold meetings, it allows restrictions on the secrecy of the mail, post and telecommunications systems, the ordering of house searches and confiscation of property and restrictions on property rights.

Decree of the Reich President (1933)

Center for Civic Education

- explain how political and economic freedoms serve to limit governmental power
- evaluate the argument that limited government is essential to the protection of political and economic freedoms

C. What are the nature and purposes of constitutions?

Content summary and rationale

The term **"constitution"** has alternative meanings, and constitutions serve differing purposes in different nations. In some a constitution is merely a description of a form of government. In others, such as the United States and France, a constitution is considered a higher law that establishes and limits government in order to protect individual rights as well as to promote the common good. In nations with unlimited governments, constitutions often have served as a cloak to misrule, disguising the unconstrained behavior of those in power.

In the United States, **constitutional government** is equated with limited government. Even in a constitutional government, however, the constitution alone cannot guarantee that the limits imposed on government will be respected or that the purposes of government will be served. There are certain social, economic, and political conditions that enable constitutional government to flourish.

To preserve and improve constitutional government, citizens must understand the necessary conditions for its existence. There must be general agreement about the proper relationship among the people, their constitution, and their government. Finally, not only must the constitution regulate institutions, the people also must cultivate a disposition to behave in ways consistent with its values and principles

Content standards

1. **Concepts of "constitution."** *Students should be able to explain different uses of the term "constitution" and to distinguish between governments with a constitution and a constitutional government.*

   To achieve this standard students should be able to
   - distinguish among the following uses of the term constitution
     - a document or collection of documents
     - a written document augmented over time by custom, legislation, and court decisions
     - a description of a form of government
     - a higher law that limits the powers of government, i.e., a constitutional (or limited) government
   - distinguish between governments with a constitution and constitutional (limited) government
   - identify historical and contemporary examples of nations that have had constitutions that do not limit power, e.g., Nazi Germany, the former Soviet Union, and the People's Republic of China; distinguish them from nations that have constitutional governments, e.g., Germany, United Kingdom, Japan, United States

2. **Purposes and uses of constitutions.** *Students should be able to explain the various purposes served by constitutions.*

   To achieve this standard, students should be able to

   ■ explain how constitutions set forth the structure of government, give the government power, and establish the relationship between the people and their government

   ■ explain how constitutions may limit government's power in order to protect individual rights and promote the common good; give historical and contemporary examples

   ■ explain how constitutions may embody the core values and principles of a political system and provide a reference point for citizens to use in evaluating the actions of their government

   ■ describe historical and contemporary instances of how constitutions have been disregarded or used to promote the interests of a particular group, class, faction, or a government itself, e.g., slavery, exclusion of women from the body politic, prohibition of competing political parties

   ■ explain how constitutions can be vehicles for change and for resolving social issues, e.g., use of the Fourteenth Amendment to the United States Constitution in the civil rights movement of the 1950s and 1960s; establishment of the Japanese Constitution after World War II, which provided women the right to vote

   ■ explain how constitutions can be devices for preserving core values and principles of a society, e.g., prohibition of religious tests for public office, protection of private property by the United States Constitution

Constitutions may embody the core values and principles of a political system and provide a reference point for citizens to use in evaluating the actions of their government.

3. **Conditions under which constitutional government flourishes.** *Students should be able to evaluate, take, and defend positions on what conditions contribute to the establishment and maintenance of constitutional government.*

   To achieve this standard, students should be able to

   ■ explain the social, economic, and political conditions that may foster constitutional government

   ■ evaluate the claim that the formal establishment of a government under a constitution is not of itself sufficient to maintain liberty

   ■ evaluate the reasons why some nations have been successful in establishing constitutional government, while others have not, e.g., post-World War II Germany, Japan (successes); Nigeria, Kenya, Argentina under Peron (failures)

   ■ identify the most important responsibilities individual citizens and people serving in government should assume to insure the preservation and improvement of constitutional government

Constitutions may limit government in order to protect individual rights and promote the common good.

D. What are alternative ways of organizing constitutional governments?

Content summary and rationale

The way a government is organized is a reflection of its most fundamental purposes. For that reason, constitutional governments organize their institutions to channel and limit the exercise of political power to serve the purposes for which they have been established.

The most common forms of organization of the institutions of central governments at the national level are **systems of shared powers** and **parliamentary systems**.

- In **systems of shared powers**, such as the United States, powers are separated among branches. Each branch has primary responsibility for certain functions, but each branch also shares these powers and functions with the others, e.g., the president, Congress, and the Supreme Court all share power over the laws of the nation.

- In **parliamentary systems** such as Great Britain, authority is held by a bicameral legislature called Parliament. Parliament consists of the House of Lords and the House of Commons. The prime minister is chosen by convention from the ranks of the majority party in Commons. The prime minister forms a cabinet and directs the administration of the government.

There are several kinds of relationships between the central government of a nation and other units of government within the nation. The most common forms of such relationships, all of which have been or can be found in the United States, are **confederal, federal, and unitary systems.**

In constitutional governments the basis of representation can vary. Representation may be based on such factors as gender, property, social class, geography, race, or religion. There are also variations in electorial systems. In some systems, electoral districts choose a single member elected by plurality or majority—winner-take-all; in other systems, electoral districts choose multiple members in proportion to the number of votes received—proportional representation.

By comparing alternative means of organizing constitutional governments and the ways they provide for representation, citizens become aware of the advantages and disadvantages of their own system and how it may be improved.

By comparing alternative means of organizing constitutional governments and the ways they provide for representation, citizens become aware of the advantages and disadvantages of their own system and how it may be improved. This understanding also provides a basis for evaluating whether one's own government is diverging from its constitutional design and purposes. This knowledge not only helps citizens to understand their own government, it enables them to grasp the meaning of events in the world, such as the fall of parliamentary governments, the breakup of federations, or the weaknesses of confederations.

Content standards

1. **Shared powers and parliamentary systems.** *Students should be able to describe the major characteristics of systems of shared powers and of parliamentary systems.*

   To achieve this standard, students should be able to

   ■ describe the major characteristics of systems of shared powers, e.g., in the United States and Brazil

   - powers are separated among branches, each branch has primary responsibility for certain functions, e.g., legislative, executive, and judicial

   - each branch also shares some of the powers and functions of the other branches, e.g.,

     - legislatures may pass laws, but the executive may veto them

     - the executive nominates certain public officials, but the legislature must approve them

     - legislatures may pass laws, but in many countries the judiciary may declare them unconstitutional

   ■ describe the major characteristics of parliamentary systems, e.g., in the United Kingdom and Israel

     - authority is held by a legislature called Parliament

     - members of Parliament are chosen in general elections, but they lose their positions at any time the government "falls" (resigns) and new elections are held

     - prime minister and cabinet may be replaced by Parliament if a majority votes "no confidence" in the government

     - the political party or parties that form a majority in Parliament choose the prime minister

     - the prime minister and members of the Cabinet must all be members of the legislature—Parliament

   ■ identify historical and contemporary examples of parliamentary systems and systems of shared powers

   ■ evaluate the various ways power is distributed, shared, and limited in systems of shared powers and parliamentary systems in terms of such criteria as effectiveness, prevention of the abuse of power, responsiveness to popular will, stability

   ■ evaluate the relative advantages and disadvantages of systems of shared powers and parliamentary systems in terms of the purposes of constitutional government

2. **Confederal, federal, and unitary systems.** *Students should be able to explain the advantages and disadvantages of federal, confederal, and unitary systems of government.*

   To achieve this standard, students should be able to

   ■ define confederal, federal, and unitary systems of government

Center for Civic Education

[A]s far as the principle...[of confederacy] has prevailed, it has been the cause of incurable disorder and imbecility in government.

Alexander Hamilton (1788)

- **confederal system**—a system of government in which sovereign states delegate powers to a central government for specific purposes, e.g., mutual defense against foreign enemies

- **federal system**—a system in which a national government shares powers with state governments, but the national government may act directly on individuals within the states, e.g., national government may require individuals to pay income taxes

- **unitary system**—a system in which all power is concentrated in a central government; state and local governments can exercise only those powers given to them by the central government

■ identify historical and contemporary examples of confederal, federal, and unitary systems

■ evaluate the various ways power is distributed, shared, and limited in confederal, federal, and unitary systems in terms of such criteria as effectiveness, prevention of the abuse of power, responsiveness to popular will, stability

■ explain the relative advantages and disadvantages of confederal, federal, and unitary systems in terms of the purposes of constitutional government

3. **Nature of representation.** *Students should be able to evaluate, take, and defend positions on how well alternative forms of representation serve the purposes of constitutional government.*

To achieve this standard, students should be able to

■ explain the major arguments for and against representative government as distinguished from direct popular rule

■ describe common bases upon which representation is or has been established, e.g.,

- geographic areas

- citizenship

- social class or caste

- age, sex, or property

- religion, race, and ethnicity

■ evaluate differing bases of electoral systems, e.g.,

- winner-take-all systems

- proportional systems

■ evaluate differing theories of representation, e.g., the theory that the foremost obligation of a representative is to promote the interests of

- a particular constituency

- the society as a whole

Your representative owes you, not his industry only, but his judgment; and he betrays instead of serving you if he sacrifices it to your opinion.

Edmund Burke (1774)

Center for Civic Education

II. WHAT ARE THE FOUNDATIONS OF THE AMERICAN POLITICAL SYSTEM?

A. What is the American idea of constitutional government?

Content summary and rationale

Using a written constitution to set forth the values and principles of government and to establish and limit its powers is among the nation's most distinctive accomplishments. The American system of government relies upon its citizens' holding these constitutional values and principles in common.

The Framers of the United States Constitution intended to establish, in the words of James Madison, an "energetic" and effective government, one capable of fulfilling the purposes for which it was created. The Constitution provides for institutions that facilitate the formation of majorities on various issues at the same time as it limits the powers of those majorities to protect the basic liberties of the people. The Bill of Rights was adopted as an additional means of limiting the powers of the national government and has become central to the American idea of constitutional government.

An understanding of the extent to which Americans have internalized the values and principles of the Constitution will contribute to an appreciation of the enduring influence of the Constitution as it has helped to shape the character of American society.

Citizens must understand the fundamental ideas of American constitutional government and their history and contemporary relevance to develop a reasoned commitment to them, as well as to use them as criteria to evaluate their own behavior and the behavior of government officials.

> *The important distinction so well understood in America between a Constitution established by the people and unalterable by the government, and a law established by the government and alterable by the government seems to have been little understood and less observed in any other country.*
>
> **James Madison (1788)**

Content standards

1. **The American idea of constitutional government.** *Students should be able to explain the central ideas of American constitutional government and their history.*

   To achieve this standard, students should be able to

   ■ describe major historical events that led to the creation of limited government in the United States, e.g.,

     ■ Magna Carta (1215), common law, and the Bill of Rights (1689) in England

     ■ colonial experience, Declaration of Independence (1776), Articles of Confederation (1781), state constitutions and charters, United States Constitution (1787), Bill of Rights (1791) in the United States

   ■ explain the importance of the central ideas of the natural rights philosophy in the creation of American constitutional government, e.g., that all persons have the right to life, liberty, property, and the pursuit of happiness just because they are human beings; that the major purpose of government is to protect those rights

> *[The government of the United States is] a government limited...by the authority of a paramount Constitution.*
>
> **James Madison (1788)**

- explain the major ideas about republican government which influenced the development of the United States Constitution, e.g., the concept of representative government, the importance of civic virtue or concern for the common good

- explain the central ideas of American constitutional government such as

  - popular sovereignty, i.e., the people as the ultimate source of the power to create, alter, or abolish governments

  - the necessity for a written constitution to set forth the organization of government and to grant and distribute its powers, e.g., among different branches of the national government, between the national government and the states, and between the people and the government

  - the Constitution as a "higher law" that authorizes and legitimizes an "energetic" and effective government of limited powers

  - the Constitution as legitimizing majority rule in certain key areas of decision making, while limiting the power of these majorities in order to protect the rights of individuals

- explain how various provisions of the Constitution and principles of the constitutional system are devices to insure an effective government that will not exceed its limits

- explain how the design of the institutions of government and the federal system channels and limits governmental power in order to serve the purposes of American constitutional democracy

2. **How American constitutional government has shaped the character of American society.** *Students should be able to explain the extent to which Americans have internalized the values and principles of the Constitution and attempted to make its ideals realities.*

To achieve this standard, students should be able to

- explain ways in which belief in limited government has influenced American society

- explain ways in which the Constitution has encouraged Americans to engage in commercial and other productive activities

- explain how major features of the Constitution, such as federalism and the Bill of Rights, have helped to shape American society

- describe, giving historical and contemporary examples, how Americans have attempted to make the values and principles of the Constitution a reality

The people made the Constitution, and the people can unmake it. It is the creature of their own will, and lives only by their will.

John Marshall (1821)

It was from America that...ideas long locked in the breast of solitary thinkers, and hidden among Latin folios— burst forth like a conqueror upon the world...and the principle gained ground, that a nation can never abandon its fate to an authority it cannot control.

Lord Acton (1907)

B. What are the distinctive characteristics of American society?

Content summary and rationale

The distinctive characteristics of American society have shaped the way Americans perceive the proper relationship among individuals, society, and the government. Americans need to know the distinctive characteristics of their society in order to know who they are—their identity as a people. This understanding of a common identity and common purposes provides a basis on which a diverse American society can work cooperatively to solve common problems and manage conflicts within constitutional boundaries.

Unlike many other nations, the United States never experienced feudalism, accepted an inherited caste system, or recognized a nobility. The existence of a frontier, large-scale and continuing immigration, and the abundance and widespread ownership of property, have fostered the growth of a democratic way of life. Notable exceptions that have worked against the attainment of social equality are the history of slavery, the treatment of Native Americans, and discrimination against various groups.

Voluntarism is another prominent characteristic of American life. The American tradition of voluntarism emerged from the colonists' dependence on one another during the early settlement period, it was enhanced by the influence of a frontier, and encouraged by Americans' religious beliefs. This propensity for voluntarism has continued to the present day and has given rise to questions that citizens need to address: Is it advantageous for society that functions such as education and social welfare be performed by voluntary associations? By government? Or should both have a role? Would American society be harmed or enhanced if the propensity to voluntarism declined?

Americans form and join associations in great numbers. The broad range of religious, service, and civic groups forms a part of the rich network of associations that characterizes American society. The powerful role of these kinds of groups, as well as interest groups, labor unions, and professional organizations, is an important factor in understanding American political life.

Recognition of the many forms of diversity in American society— ethnicity, race, religion, class, language, gender, or national origin—embraced in a constitutional system, is a prerequisite to making judgments about the benefits diversity offers and the challenges it poses.

Content standards

1. **Distinctive characteristics of American society**. *Students should be able to explain how the following characteristics tend to distinguish American society from most other societies.*

   To achieve this standard, students should be able to

   - explain important factors that have helped shape American society, such as

     - absence of a nobility or an inherited caste system

     - religious freedom

     - a history of slavery

The one absolutely certain way of bringing this nation to ruin, of preventing all possibility of its continuing to be a nation at all would be to permit it to become a tangle of squabbling nationalities...each preserving its separate nationality.
   Theodore Roosevelt (1910)

Democracy is still upon its trial. The civic genius of our people is its only bulwark.
   William James (1897)

Center for Civic Education

- the Judeo-Christian ethic
- relative geographic isolation
- abundance of land and widespread ownership of property
- social, economic, and geographic mobility
- effects of a frontier
- large scale immigration
- diversity of the population
- individualism
- work ethic
- market economy
- relative social equality
- universal public education

■ compare the distinctive characteristics of American society with those of other countries

Americans of all ages, all stations in life, and all types of disposition are forever forming associations...at the head of any new undertaking, where in France you would find the government or in England some territorial magnate, in the United States you are sure to find as association.

Alexis de Tocqueville (1835)

2. **The role of voluntarism in American life.** *Students should be able to evaluate, take, and defend positions on the importance of voluntarism in American society.*

To achieve this standard, students should be able to

■ explain factors that have inclined Americans toward voluntarism, e.g., colonial conditions, the Puritan ethic, frontier traditions, religious beliefs

■ describe the role of voluntary associations in performing functions usually associated with government, such as providing social welfare and education; give historical and contemporary examples

■ describe the extent of voluntarism in American society compared to other countries

■ explain the relationship of voluntarism to Americans' ideas about limited government

■ evaluate arguments regarding what responsibilities properly belong to individuals or to groups and to the private sector or to the government and how these responsibilities should be shared by the private sector and government

3. **The role of organized groups in political life.** *Students should be able to evaluate, take, and defend positions on the contemporary role of organized groups in American social and political life.*

To achieve this standard, students should be able to

■ identify examples of organized groups and discuss their historical and contemporary role in local, state, and national politics, e.g., unions, professional organizations; religious, charitable, service, and civic groups

■ describe and evaluate the role of organized groups in performing functions usually associated with government, such as providing social welfare and education

4. **Diversity in American society.** *Students should be able to evaluate, take and defend positions on issues regarding diversity in American life.*

To achieve this standard, students should be able to

■ identify the many forms of diversity found in American society, e.g., racial, religious, ethnic, socioeconomic, regional, linguistic

■ explain the impact on American politics, both historically and at present, of the racial, religious, socioeconomic, regional, ethnic, and linguistic diversity of American society

■ explain alternative ideas about the role and value of diversity in American life both historically and at present

■ describe conflicts that have arisen from diversity and explain the means by which some have been managed and explain why some conflicts have persisted unabated

■ explain the importance of adhering to constitutional values and principles in managing conflicts over diversity

America is woven of many strands; I would recognize them and let it so remain....Our fate is to become one and yet many.
Ralph Ellison (1952)

C. What is American political culture?

Content summary and rationale

In contrast to most other nations, the identity of an American citizen is defined by shared political values and principles rather than by ethnicity, race, religion, class, language, gender, or national origin. These shared values and principles have helped to promote cohesion in the daily life of Americans and in times of crisis have enabled them to find common ground with those who differ from them.

Although political conflicts sometimes have erupted in violence, such as labor disputes, race riots, and draft riots, citizens should understand that political conflict in the United States has usually been less divisive and violent than in many other nations. This is in part because American political conflict, with the major exception of the Civil War, has generally taken place within a constitutional framework which allows for protest politics and promotes the peaceful resolution of differences.

To understand their nation, citizens should appreciate the nature and importance of their political culture, which provides a foundation for the stability of their system, and its capacity to respond to the needs and interests of the people through peaceful change.

The principle on which this country was founded and by which it has always been governed is that Americanism is a matter of the mind and heart; Americanism is not, and never was, a matter of race and ancestry. A good American is one who is loyal to this country and to our creed of liberty and democracy.
Franklin Delano Roosevelt (1943)

Content standards

1. **American national identity and political culture.** *Students should be able to explain the importance of shared political and civic beliefs and values to the maintenance of constitutional democracy in an increasingly diverse American society.*

To achieve this standard, students should be able to

■ explain that shared political and civic beliefs and values define an American citizen rather than ethnicity, race, religion, class, language, gender, or national origin

Here, in the first paragraph of the Declaration [of Independence], is the assertion of the natural right of all to the ballot; for how can "the consent of the governed" be given, if the right to vote be denied?

Susan B. Anthony (1873)

- explain the shared ideas and values of American political culture as set forth in

  - basic documents such as the Declaration of Independence, the United States Constitution and Bill of Rights

  - other sources such as *The Federalist* and Anti-federalist writings, the Declaration of Sentiments of the Seneca Falls Convention of 1848, Abraham Lincoln's "Gettysburg Address," Woodrow Wilson's "Fourteen Points," Franklin Roosevelt's "Four Freedoms," Martin Luther King's "Letter from the Birmingham Jail," and many landmark decisions of the Supreme Court of the United States

- describe beliefs common to American political culture, such as the belief in equality of opportunity; mistrust of power, as well as high expectations of what elected officials and government should do; the need to admit to faults or shortcomings in their society; and the belief that they can individually and through collective effort alleviate social, economic, or political problems

2. **Character of American political conflict.** *Students should be able to describe the character of American political conflict and explain factors that usually tend to prevent it or lower its intensity.*

To achieve this standard, students should be able to

- describe political conflict in the United States both historically and at present, such as conflict about

  - geographic or sectional interests

  - slavery and indentured servitude

  - national origins

  - extending the franchise

  - extending civil rights to all Americans

  - the role of religion in American public life

  - the rights of organized labor

  - the role of government in regulating business

  - engaging in wars

- explain some of the reasons why political conflict in the United States, with notable exceptions such as the Civil War, nineteenth century labor unrest, the 1950s and 1960s civil rights struggles, and the opposition to the war in Vietnam, has generally been less divisive than in many other nations. These include

  - a shared respect for the Constitution and its principles

  - the existence of many opportunities to influence government and to participate in it

  - the concept of a loyal opposition

  - willingness to relinquish power when voted out of office

  - acceptance of majority rule tempered by respect for minority rights

  - recourse to the legal system to manage conflicts

Here in America we are descended in blood and spirit from revolutionists and rebels—men and women who dare to dissent from accepted doctrine. As their heirs, we may never confuse honest dissent with disloyal subversion.

Dwight D. Eisenhower (1954)

Center for Civic Education

- availability of land and abundance of natural resources

- a relatively high standard of living

- opportunities to improve one's economic condition

- opportunities for free, public education

- a sense of unity within diversity

■ explain the ways in which universal public education and the existence of a popular culture that crosses class boundaries have tended to reduce the intensity of political conflict by creating common ground among diverse groups

D. What values and principles are basic to American constitutional democracy?

Content summary and rationale

The constitutional values and principles held by Americans provide the foundation for their attitudes regarding the proper ends and means of political life. They have shaped American political institutions and practices.

In addition to experience, several intellectual traditions have influenced the development of American constitutional democracy. Among the most important of these were the ideas of **classical liberalism** with its emphasis on individual rights and **classical republicanism**. Throughout most of our history, the ideas associated with liberalism have been dominant. These ideas emerged in the seventeenth century and were further developed during the eighteenth-century Enlightenment. The view that the individual, possessing certain inalienable rights, is the basic unit of society is the fundamental element of classical liberal thought. Classical liberalism includes the ideas that governments are created by the people to protect their inalienable rights to life, liberty, and property and derive their authority from the consent of the governed. The Declaration of Independence is a succinct statement of the central ideas of classical liberalism.

Two central ideas of classical republicanism are the concepts of **civic virtue** and the **common good**. Civic virtue requires the individual to subordinate personal interests to the interests of the community as a whole—the common good. Republicanism considers promotion of the common good—the good of the people as a whole rather than the good of the individual or of certain segments of society—to be the fundamental purpose of government. This purpose is reflected in the Preamble to the Constitution and the body of the Constitution. Classical republicanism, like democracy, includes the idea of rule by the people exercised directly or indirectly through representatives.

The values and principles of American constitutional democracy are sometimes in conflict, and their very meaning and application are often disputed. For example, although most Americans agree that the idea of equality is an important value, they may disagree about what priority it should be given in comparison with other values such as liberty. And they may disagree on the meaning of equality when it is applied to a specific situation. To participate constructively in public debate concerning fundamental values and principles, citizens need to understand them sufficiently.

A thirst for liberty seems to be the ruling passion not only of America but of the present age.
Thomas Hutchinson (1711)

The republican is the only form of government which is not eternally at open or secret war with the rights of mankind.
Thomas Jefferson (1790)

Disparities have always existed between the realities of daily life and the ideals of American constitutional democracy. The history of the United States, however, has been marked by continuing attempts to narrow the gap between these ideals and reality. For these reasons, Americans have united in political movements to abolish slavery, extend the franchise, remove legal support for segregation, and provide equality of opportunity for each individual. Citizens must be aware of historical and contemporary efforts in which Americans have joined forces to achieve this end.

Citizens, therefore, need to understand that American society is perpetually "unfinished" and that each generation must address ways to narrow the disparity between ideals and reality.

The Spirit that prevails among Men of all degrees, all ages and sexes is the Spirit of Liberty
Abigail Adams (1775)

Content standards

1. **Liberalism and American constitutional democracy.** *Students should be able to explain the meaning of the terms "liberal" and "democracy" in the phrase "liberal democracy."*

   To achieve this standard, students should be able to

   ■ explain that the term "liberal" is derived from "liberty" and refers to a form of government in which individual rights and freedoms are protected

      ■ explain that the term liberal has its historical roots in the ideas of liberalism that emerged in the seventeenth century and developed during the eighteenth-century Enlightenment

      ■ explain the relationship between liberalism and the Protestant Reformation and the rise of market economies and free enterprise

      ■ explain that the central idea of liberalism is a belief that the individual has rights which exist independently of government and which ought to be protected by and against government

      ■ explain the difference between the use of the term "liberal" when it is referring to the American form of government and the use of the terms "liberal" and "conservative" in referring to positions on the spectrum of American politics

   ■ explain that the term "democracy" is derived from the Greek word for "rule by the people"

      ■ explain that the central focus of democracy is that the people are the source of authority for government and how that idea is related to free elections and widespread participation

As I would not be a slave, so I would not be a master. This expresses my idea of democracy. Whatever differs from this, to the extent of the difference, is no democracy.
Abraham Lincoln (1858)

      ■ explain the difference between the use of the term "democratic" to refer to the American form of government and the use of the term to refer to the Democratic Party in the United States

   ■ explain how the basic premises of liberalism and democracy are joined in the Declaration of Independence, where they are stated as "self-evident Truths," i.e.,

      ■ "all men are created equal"

      ■ "they are endowed...with certain unalienable rights"

      ■ governments are artificial—they "are instituted among men"

Center for Civic Education

- people have a right to create a government to protect their rights

- governments are established for the limited purposes of securing individual rights

- authority is derived from consent of the governed

- people have the right to alter or abolish government when it fails to fulfill its purposes

2. **Republicanism and American constitutional democracy**. *Students should be able to explain how and why ideas of classical republicanism are reflected in the values and principles of American constitutional democracy.*

To achieve this standard, students should be able to

- define a "republic" as a state in which the citizenry as a whole is considered sovereign but which is governed by elected representatives rather than directly by the people, as in direct democracy

- explain major ideas of republicanism, i.e.,

  - government of a republic seeks the public or common good rather than the good of a particular group or class of society

  - "civic virtue" of citizens is essential; civic virtue means that citizens put the public or common good above their private interests

- explain how ideas of classical republicanism are reflected in the United States Constitution, e.g., in the Preamble, the guarantee to the states of a "republican form of government" in (Article IV Section 4) provisions for the election of representatives to the Congress in Article I Section 2 and the Seventeenth Amendment

- explain the difference between the use of the term "republican" to refer to the American form of government and the use of the term to refer to the Republican Party in the United States

- explain why classical republicanism and liberalism are potentially in conflict, e.g., the primary purpose of government—promotion of the public or common good vs. protection of individual rights

- evaluate, take, and defend positions on the importance of civic virtue for American democracy today

3. **Fundamental values and principles**. *Students should be able to evaluate, take, and defend positions on what the fundamental values and principles of American political life are and their importance to the maintenance of constitutional democracy.*

To achieve this standard, students should be able to

- explain the following values which are widely considered to be fundamental to American civic life

  - individual rights, i.e., life, liberty, property, and the pursuit of happiness

  - the public or common good

> *The Government of the Union, then, is emphatically and truly a government of the people. In form and in substance it emanates from them. Its powers are granted by them, and are to be exercised directly on them and for their benefit.*
>
> **John Marshall (1819)**

> *The life of a republic lies certainly in the energy, virtue, and intelligence of its citizens.*
>
> **Andrew Johnson (1865)**

Center for Civic Education

- self government
- justice
- equality
- diversity
- openness and free inquiry
- truth
- patriotism

■ explain the following principles widely considered to be fundamental to American constitutional democracy

- popular sovereignty—the concept that ultimate political authority rests with the people who create and can alter or abolish governments
- constitutional government, including
  - rule of law
  - representative institutions
  - separated and shared powers
  - checks and balances
  - individual rights
  - separation of church and state
  - federalism
  - civilian control of the military

■ identify the fundamental values and principles expressed in basic documents, significant political speeches and writings, and the individual and group actions that embody them

■ explain how the institutions of government reflect fundamental values and principles, e.g., justice, equality, the common good, popular sovereignty, checks and balances

■ explain the interdependence among certain values and principles, e.g., individual liberty and diversity

■ explain the significance of fundamental values and principles for the individual and society

4. **Conflicts among values and principles in American political and social life.** *Students should be able to evaluate, take, and defend positions on issues in which fundamental values and principles may be in conflict.*

To achieve this standard, students should be able to

■ describe historical and contemporary issues which involve conflicts among fundamental values and principles and explain how these conflicts might be resolved

- liberty and equality
- liberty and authority
- individual rights and the common good

Let me be a free man— free to travel, free to stop, free to work, free to trade where I choose, free to choose my own teachers, free to follow the religion of my fathers, free to think and talk and act for myself— and I will obey every law, or submit to the penalty.
Chief Joseph (1879)

I contend that woman has just as much right to sit in solemn counsel in conventions, conferences, associations and general assemblies, as man—just as much right to sit upon the throne of England or in the Presidential chair of the United States.
Angelina Grimke (1837)

Center for Civic Education

■ explain why people may agree on values or principles in the abstract but disagree when they are applied to specific issues, e.g., the right to life and capital punishment

5. **Disparities between ideals and reality in American political and social life**. *Students should be able to evaluate, take, and defend positions about issues concerning the disparities between American ideals and realities.*

To achieve this standard, students should be able to

■ explain the importance of Americans' establishing ideals in political life and their insistence on comparing current practices with these ideals

■ explain, using historical and contemporary examples, discrepancies between American ideals and the realities of American social and political life, e.g., the ideal of equal opportunity and the reality of unfair discrimination

■ describe historical and contemporary efforts to reduce discrepancies between ideals and reality in American public life, e.g., abolitionists; suffrage, union, and civil rights movements; government programs such as Head Start; civil rights legislation and enforcement

■ explain ways in which discrepancies between reality and the ideals of American constitutional democracy can be reduced by

   ■ individual action

   ■ social action

   ■ political action

I have a dream that my four little children will one day live in a nation where they will not be judged by the color of their skin but by the content of their character.
Martin Luther King, Jr. (1963)

Center for Civic Education

The people, sir, erected this government. They gave it a constitution, and in that constitution they have enumerated the powers which they bestow on it. They have made it a limited government.

Daniel Webster (1830)

III. HOW DOES THE GOVERNMENT ESTABLISHED BY THE CONSTITUTION EMBODY THE PURPOSES, VALUES, AND PRINCIPLES OF AMERICAN DEMOCRACY?

A. How are power and responsibility distributed, shared, and limited in the government established by the United States Constitution?

Content summary and rationale

The system of government established by the Constitution has resulted in a complex dispersal of powers. As a result, every American lives under the jurisdiction of national, state, and local governments, all of whose powers and responsibilities are separated and shared among different branches and agencies.

All these governments—national, state, and local—affect the daily life of every American. This complex system of multiple levels and divisions of government is difficult to understand and is sometimes inefficient. It may result in delaying or preventing actions which may or may not be desirable. However, this system was seen by the Framers of the Constitution as a principal means of limiting the power of government. It also provides numerous opportunities for citizens to participate in their own governance. It reflects the principle of popular sovereignty, enables citizens to hold their governments accountable, and helps to insure protection for the rights of the people.

Citizens who understand the reasons for this system of dispersed power and its design are able to evaluate, to monitor, and to influence it effectively.

Content standards

1. **Distributing governmental power and preventing its abuse**. *Students should be able to explain how the United States Constitution grants and distributes power to national and state government and how it seeks to prevent the abuse of power.*

   To achieve this standard, students should be able to

   - explain how the overall design and specific features of the Constitution are intended to

     - aggregate power at different levels to allow government to be responsive and effective, e.g., powers granted to Congress in Article I, Section 8

     - disperse power among different levels of government to reduce chances of its abuse, protect individual rights and promote the common good

     - balance and check powers to prevent their abuse, e.g., separated institutions with shared powers, provisions for veto and impeachment, federalism, judicial review, separation of church and state, subordination of the military to civilian control, the Bill of Rights

Constitutions are checks upon the hasty action of the majority. They are the self-imposed restraints of a whole people upon a majority of them to secure sober action and a respect for the rights of the minority.

William Howard Taft (c.1900)

Center for Civic Education

2. **The American federal system**. *Students should be able to evaluate, take, and defend positions on issues regarding the distribution of powers and responsibilities within the federal system.*

To achieve this standard, students should be able to

- explain why the Framers adopted a federal system in which power and responsibility are divided and shared between a national government, having certain nationwide responsibilities, and state governments having state and local responsibilities

- explain how the Constitution's overall design and specific features were intended to place limitations on both national and state governments, e.g., states cannot restrict interstate commerce

- explain how the federal system provides numerous opportunities for citizens to participate through its dispersal of power among and between

  - national, state, and local governments

  - branches and agencies of the national, state, and local governments

- explain how the federal system provides numerous opportunities for citizens to hold their governments accountable

- explain ways in which federalism is designed to protect individual rights to life, liberty, and property and how it has at times made it possible for states to deny the rights of certain groups, e.g., states' rights and slavery, denial of suffrage to women and minority groups

- describe historical conflicts over the respective roles of national and state governments and the importance of the Tenth Amendment

- evaluate the respective roles of national and state governments in the contemporary federal system

The question of the relation of the states to the federal government is the cardinal question of our constitutional system....It cannot, indeed, be settled by the opinion of any one generation.
Woodrow Wilson (1908)

B. How is the national government organized and what does it do?

Content summary and rationale

The actions of the national government have significant consequences on the daily lives of all Americans, their communities, and the welfare of the nation as a whole. These actions affect their security, their standard of living, and the taxes they will pay.

To understand the impact of the national government on their daily lives and the lives of their communities, citizens need to understand how it functions. To deliberate with other citizens about political action and to influence governmental actions that affect their lives, citizens need to know the distribution of responsibilities among the various branches and agencies of government and where and how decisions are made.

The power vested in the American courts of justice of pronouncing a statute to be unconstitutional forms one of the most powerful barriers that have ever been devised against the tyranny of political assemblies.

Alexis de Tocqueville (1835)

Content standards

1. **The institutions of the national government.** *Students should be able to evaluate, take, and defend positions on issues regarding the purposes, organization, and functions of the institutions of the national government.*

   To achieve this standard, students should be able to

   - describe the purposes, organization, and functions of the three branches of the national government

     - **legislative**, i.e., the Congress, composed of a House of Representatives and a Senate, including their committees and their respective staffs and most prominent auxiliary agencies, e.g., the Congressional Budget Office, Library of Congress

     - **executive**, including its most prominent agencies, e.g., State, Defense, Health and Human Services, Justice, Education

     - **judicial**, including the Supreme Court of the United States and the federal court system

     - **independent regulatory agencies**, e.g., Federal Reserve Board, Food and Drug Administration, Federal Communications Commission

   - evaluate the extent to which each branch of the government reflects the people's sovereignty, e.g., Congress legislates on behalf of the people, the president represents the people as a nation, the Supreme Court acts on behalf of the people as a whole when it interprets their Constitution

   - explain why certain provisions of the Constitution result in tensions among the three branches of government, e.g., the power of the purse, the power of impeachment, advice and consent, veto power, judicial review

   - explain how and why beliefs about the purposes and functions of the national government have changed over time

   - evaluate the argument that separation of powers, checks and balances, and judicial review tend to slow down the process of making and enforcing laws, thus insuring better outcomes

   - evaluate current issues concerning representation, e.g., term limitations, legislative districting, geographical and group representation

2. **Major responsibilities of the national government in domestic and foreign policy.** *Students should be able to evaluate, take, and defend positions on issues regarding the major responsibilities of the national government for domestic and foreign policy.*

   To achieve this standard, students should be able to

   - explain the major responsibilities of the national government for domestic policy and how domestic policies affect their everyday lives and their community

- explain the major responsibilities of the national government for foreign policy and how foreign policies, including trade policy and national security, affect their everyday lives and their community

- evaluate competing arguments about the proper role of government in major areas of domestic and foreign policy, e.g., health care, education, child care, regulation of business and industry, foreign aid, intervention abroad

3. **Financing government through taxation.** *Students should be able to evaluate, take, and defend positions on issues regarding how government should raise money to pay for its operations and services.*

To achieve this standard, students should be able to

- explain the history of taxation in the United States and why taxation is necessary to pay for government

- explain provisions of the United States Constitution that authorize the national government to collect taxes, i.e., Article I, Sections 7 and 8, Sixteenth Amendment

- identify major sources of revenue for the national government, e.g., individual income taxes, social insurance receipts (Social Security and Medicare), borrowing, taxes on corporations and businesses, estate and excise taxes

- identify major uses of tax revenues received by the national government, e.g., direct payment to individuals (Social Security, Medicaid, Medicare, Aid to Families with Dependent Children), interstate highways, national defense, interest on the federal debt, national parks

- explain why there is often a tension between citizens' desire for government services and benefits and their unwillingness to pay taxes for them

- evaluate the equity of various kinds of taxes

Taxes are what we pay for civilized society.
Oliver Wendell Holmes, Jr. (1904)

C. How are state and local governments organized and what do they do?

Content summary and rationale

State governments are established by state constitutions. Each has its own legislative, executive, and judicial branch. States possess substantial powers that, along with their local and intermediate governments, affect citizens' lives from birth to death.

Local governments provide most of the services citizens receive, and local courts handle most civil disputes and violations of the law. State and local governments license businesses, professions, automobiles, and drivers; provide essential services such as police and fire protection, education, and street maintenance; regulate zoning and the construction of buildings; provide public housing, transportation, and public health services; and maintain streets, highways, airports, and harbors.

Because of their geographic location and the fact that their meetings usually are open to the public, state and local governments are often quite accessible to the people. Members of city councils, boards of education, mayors, governors, and other officials are often available to meet with individuals and groups and to speak to students and civic organizations.

Citizens need to know the purposes, organization, and responsibilities of their state and local governments so they can take part in their governance.

Content standards

1. **The constitutional status of state and local governments.** *Students should be able to evaluate, take, and defend positions on issues regarding the proper relationship between the national government and the state and local governments.*

To achieve this standard, students should be able to

- describe similarities and differences between their state constitution and the federal constitution

- describe the limits the United States Constitution places on the powers of the states, e.g., coining money, prohibitions against impairing interstate commerce, making treaties with foreign governments, restrictions imposed by the Fourteenth Amendment and the Bill of Rights through the process of incorporation

- describe the limits the United States Constitution places on the powers of the national government over state governments, e.g., the national government cannot abolish a state, the Tenth Amendment to the Constitution reserves certain powers to the states

- identify powers most commonly associated with state governments

    - **reserved powers**—powers not delegated to the national government or prohibited to states by the United States Constitution, e.g., legislation regarding public safety, marriage and divorce; education; the conduct of elections; chartering regional and local governments; licensing drivers, businesses, and professions

    - **concurrent powers**—powers jointly held with the national government, e.g., legislating taxation, regulating trade and industry, borrowing money, maintaining courts, protecting the environment

- explain how the citizens of a state can change their state constitution and give examples of such changes in their own state

- evaluate changes that have taken place in the relationship between state and local governments and the national government

- evaluate the argument that state and local governments provide significant opportunities for experimentation and innovation

The proposed Constitution, so far from implying an abolition of the State Governments, makes them constituent parts of the national sovereignty...and leaves in their possession certain exclusive and very important portions of sovereign power. This fully corresponds, in every rational import of the terms with the idea of a Federal Government

Alexander Hamilton (1787)

2. **Organization of state and local governments**. *Students should be able to evaluate, take, and defend positions on issues regarding the relationships between state and local governments and citizen access to those governments.*

    To achieve this standard, students should be able to

    ■   describe how their state and local governments are organized, e.g., the organization of legislative, executive, and judicial functions at state and local levels

    ■   evaluate the relationship between their state and local governments

    ■   explain how the policies of state and local governments provide citizens ways to monitor and influence their actions and hold members of government accountable, e.g., requirements of fair and public notice of meetings, meetings of government agencies must be open to the public, public trials, provision of opportunities for citizens to be heard

3. **Major responsibilities of state and local governments.** *Students should be able to identify the major responsibilities of their state and local governments and evaluate how well they are being fulfilled.*

    To achieve this standard, students should be able to

    ■   identify the major responsibilities of their state and local governments and explain how those governments affect their lives

    ■   identify the major sources of revenue for state and local governments, e.g., property, sales, and income taxes; fees and licenses; taxes on corporations and businesses; inheritance taxes

    ■   evaluate the equity of major sources of revenue for state and local governments

D. What is the place of law in the American constitutional system?

Content summary and rationale

The rule of law operates within a framework provided by the United States Constitution. It establishes limits on both those who govern and the governed, making possible a system of ordered liberty which protects the basic rights of citizens and promotes the common good. This basic notion of the rule of law has been accompanied by the ideal of equal protection of the law, a central theme in the history of the United States.

Law pervades American society. Americans look to the principal varieties of law—constitutional, civil, and criminal—for the protection of their rights to life, liberty, and property. It is often argued, however, that Americans are overly dependent on the legal system to manage disputes about social, economic, and political problems rather than using other means available to them such as private negotiations and participation in the political process.

> *The support of State governments in all their rights, as the most competent administration of our domestic concerns, are the surest bulwarks against anti-republican tendencies.*
> **Thomas Jefferson (1801)**

> *Americans look to the principal varieties of law—constitutional, civil, and criminal— for the protection of their rights to life, liberty, and property.*

An understanding of the place of law in the American constitutional system enhances citizens' capacity to appreciate the importance of law in protecting individual rights and promoting the common good. This understanding provides a basis for deciding whether to support new laws and changes in existing law.

Content standards

All persons shall be entitled to the full and equal enjoyment of the goods, services, facilities, privileges, advantages, and accommodations of any place of public accommodation, as defined in this section, without discrimination or segregation on the ground of race, color, religion, or national origin.

Civil Rights Act of 1964

1. **The place of law in American society.** *Students should be able to evaluate, take, and defend positions on the role and importance of law in the American political system.*

To achieve this standard, students should be able to

- explain why the rule of law has a central place in American society, e.g., it
    - establishes limits on both those who govern and the governed
    - makes possible a system of ordered liberty that protects the basic rights of citizens
    - promotes the common good.
- describe historical and contemporary events and practices that illustrate the central place of the rule of law, e.g.,
    - **events**, e.g., U.S. Supreme Court cases such as *Marbury v. Madison, Brown v. Board of Education, U.S. v. Nixon*
    - **practices**, e.g., submitting bills to legal counsel to insure congressional compliance with constitutional limitations, higher court review of lower court compliance with the law, executive branch compliance with laws enacted by Congress
- describe historical and contemporary events and practices that illustrate the absence or breakdown of the rule of law, e.g.,
    - **events**, e.g., vigilantism in the early West, Ku Klux Klan attacks, urban riots, corruption in government and business, police corruption, organized crime
    - **practices**, e.g., illegal searches and seizures, bribery, interfering with the right to vote, perjury

Separate educational facilities are inherently unequal....[We] hold that the plaintiffs... [are] deprived of the equal protection of the laws guaranteed by the Fourteenth Amendment.

Earl Warren (1954)

- explain, using historical and contemporary examples, the meaning and significance of the idea of equal protection of the laws for all persons, e.g., the Fourteenth Amendment, Americans with Disabilities Act, equal opportunity legislation
- explain how the individual's rights to life, liberty, and property are protected by the trial and appellate levels of the judicial process and by the principal varieties of law, e.g., constitutional, criminal, and civil law
- evaluate the argument that Americans depend too much on the legal system to solve social, economic, and political problems rather than using other means, such as private negotiations, mediation, and participation in the political process

2. **Judicial protection of the rights of individuals.** *Students should be able to evaluate, take, and defend positions on current issues regarding the judicial protection of individual rights.*

To achieve this standard, students should be able to

■ explain the importance of an independent judiciary in a constitutional democracy

■ explain the importance of the right to due process of law for individuals accused of crimes, e.g., habeas corpus, presumption of innocence, impartial tribunal, trial by jury, right to counsel, right against self-incrimination, protection against double jeopardy, right of appeal

■ describe historical and contemporary instances in which judicial protections have not been extended to all persons

■ describe historical and contemporary instances in which judicial protections have been extended to those deprived of them in the past

■ explain why due process rights in administrative and legislative procedures are essential for the protection of individual rights and the maintenance of limited government

■ explain major means of conflict resolution, including negotiation, arbitration, mediation, and litigation and their advantages and disadvantages

■ describe the adversary system and evaluate its advantages and disadvantages

■ explain how the state and federal courts' power of judicial review reflects the American idea of constitutional government, i.e., limited government

■ evaluate arguments for and against the power of judicial review

If the meanest man in the republic is deprived of his rights, then every man in the republic is deprived of his rights.
Jane Addams (1903)

E. How does the American political system provide for choice and opportunities for participation?

Content summary and rationale

The American political system provides citizens with numerous opportunities for choice and participation. The formal institutions and processes of government such as political parties, campaigns, and elections are important avenues for choice and citizen participation. Another equally important avenue is the many associations and groups that constitute civil society. All provide ways for citizens to monitor and influence the political process.

American constitutional democracy is dynamic and sometimes disorderly. The political process is complex and does not always operate in a smooth and predictable manner. Individually and in groups, citizens attempt to influence those in power. In turn, those in power attempt to influence citizens. In this process, the public agenda—the most pressing issues of the day—is set, and public opinion regarding these issues is formed.

Morality cannot be legislated, but behavior can be regulated. Judicial decrees may not change the heart, but they can restrain the heartless.
Martin Luther King, Jr. (1963)

Center for Civic Education

If citizens do not understand the political process and how to participate in it effectively, they may feel overwhelmed and alienated. An understanding of the political process is a necessary prerequisite for effective and responsible participation in the making of public policy.

Content standards

1. **The public agenda.** *Students should be able to evaluate, take, and defend positions about how the public agenda is set.*

   To achieve this standard, students should be able to

   - explain that the "public agenda" consists of those matters that occupy public attention at any particular time, e.g., crime, health care, education, abortion, national debt, environmental protection, international intervention

   - describe how the public agenda is shaped by political leaders, political institutions, political parties, interest groups, the media, individual citizens

   - explain how individuals can help to shape the public agenda, e.g., joining interest groups or political parties, making presentations at public meetings, writing letters to newspapers and government officials

   - explain why issues important to some groups and the nation do not become a part of the public agenda

2. **Public opinion and behavior of the electorate.** *Students should be able to evaluate, take, and defend positions about the role of public opinion in American politics.*

   To achieve this standard, students should be able to

   - explain the concept of public opinion and alternative views of the proper role of public opinion in a democracy

   - explain how public opinion is measured, used in public debate, and sometimes can be manipulated

   - evaluate ways that government and the media influence public opinion

   - evaluate the influence of public opinion on public policy and the behavior of public officials

3. **Political communication: television, radio, the press, and political persuasion.** *Students should be able to evaluate, take, and defend positions on the influence of the media on American political life.*

   To achieve this standard, students should be able to

   - explain the meaning and importance of freedom of the press

   - evaluate the role of television, radio, the press, newsletters, and emerging means of communication in American politics

   - compare and contrast various forms of political persuasion and discuss the extent to which traditional forms have been replaced by electronic media

Public opinion sets bounds to every government and is the real sovereign in every free one.
James Madison (1791)

Whenever conditions are equal, public opinion brings immense weight to bear on every individual. It surrounds, directs, and oppresses him. The basic constitution of society has more to do with this than any political laws. The more alike men are, the weaker each feels in the face of all.
Alexis de Tocqueville (1835)

I fear three newspapers more than a hundred bayonets.
Napoleon Bonaparte (c. 1800)

 Center for Civic Education

- explain how Congress, the president, and state and local public officials use the media to communicate with the citizenry

- evaluate historical and contemporary political communication using such criteria as logical validity, factual accuracy, emotional appeal, distorted evidence, appeals to bias or prejudice, e.g.,

    - speeches such as Lincoln's "House Divided," Sojourner Truth's "Ain't I a Woman?", Chief Joseph's "I Shall Fight No More Forever," Roosevelt's "Four Freedoms," Martin Luther King Jr.'s "I Have a Dream"

    - government wartime information programs, campaign advertisements

    - political cartoons

4. **Political parties, campaigns, and elections**. *Students should be able to evaluate, take, and defend positions about the roles of political parties, campaigns, and elections in American politics.*

To achieve this standard, students should be able to

- describe the origins and development of the two party system in the United States

- evaluate the role of third parties in the United States

- explain how and why American political parties differ from ideological parties in other countries

- explain the major characteristics of American political parties, how they vary by locality, and how they reflect the dispersion of power providing citizens numerous opportunities for participation

- describe the role of political parties in channeling public opinion, allowing people to act jointly, nominating candidates, conducting campaigns, and training future leaders

- explain why political parties in the United States are weaker today than they have been at some times in the past

- describe varied types of elections, e.g., primary and general, local and state, congressional and presidential, initiative, referendum, recall

- evaluate the significance of campaigns and elections in the American political system

- evaluate current criticisms of campaigns and proposals for their reform

5. **Associations and groups**. *Students should be able to evaluate, take, and defend positions about the contemporary roles of associations and groups in American politics.*

To achieve this standard, students should be able to

- identify and explain the historical role of various associations and groups active in American politics, e.g., political organizations, political action committees (PACs), interest groups, voluntary and civic associations, professional organizations, unions, religious groups

Whatever facilitates a general intercourse of sentiments, as good roads, domestic commerce, a free press, and particularly a circulation of newspapers through the entire body of people...is favorable to liberty.
James Madison (1788)

The future of this republic is in the hands of the American voter.
Dwight D. Eisenhower (1949)

Political parties serve to keep each other in check, one keenly watching the other.
Henry Clay (c.1840)

Better use has been made of association and this powerful instrument of action has been applied for more varied aims in America than anywhere else in the world.
Alexis de Tocqueville (1835)

Center for Civic Education

- describe, giving historical and contemporary examples, the role of associations and groups in performing functions otherwise performed by government, such as social welfare and education
- describe the contemporary roles of associations and groups in local, state, and national politics
- evaluate the degree to which associations and groups enhance citizen participation in American political life

6. **Forming and carrying out public policy.** *Students should be able to evaluate, take, and defend positions about the formation and implementation of public policy.*

   To achieve this standard, students should be able to

   - describe a current issue of public policy at local, state, or national level
     - identify the major groups interested in that issue and explain their positions
     - identify the points at which citizens can monitor or influence the process of public policy formation
     - explain the processes by which public policy concerning that issue is formed and carried out
   - explain why conflicts about values, principles, and interests may make agreement difficult or impossible on certain issues of public policy, e.g., affirmative action, abortion, environment, gun control, capital punishment

IV. WHAT IS THE RELATIONSHIP OF THE UNITED STATES TO OTHER NATIONS AND TO WORLD AFFAIRS?

A. How is the world organized politically?

Content summary and rationale

The world is divided into **nation-states** that claim sovereignty over a defined territory and jurisdiction over everyone within it. These nation-states interact using diplomacy, formal agreements, and sanctions which may be peaceful or involve the use of force.

At the international level there is no political organization with power comparable to that of the nation-state to enforce agreements. As a result, when interests among nation-states clash, wars may erupt.

There are, however, international governmental organizations that provide avenues through which nation-states interact and attempt to manage conflicts peacefully. In addition, numerous nongovernmental organizations play increasingly important roles.

To make judgments about the role of the United States in the world today and what course American foreign policy should take, citizens need to understand some of the major elements of international relations and how world affairs affect them.

Content standards

1. **Nation-states**. *Students should be able to explain how the world is organized politically.*

   To achieve this standard, students should be able to

   ■ explain the division of the world into nation-states that claim sovereignty over a defined territory and jurisdiction over everyone within it

   ■ explain why there is no political organization at the international level with power comparable to that of the nation-state

2. **Interactions among nation-states**. *Students should be able to explain how nation-states interact with each other.*

   To achieve this standard, students should be able to

   ■ describe the most important means nation-states use to interact with one another

     ■ trade

     ■ diplomacy

     ■ treaties, agreements

     ■ international law

     ■ economic incentives and sanctions

     ■ military force and the threat of force

The world is divided into nation-states that claim sovereignty over a defined territory and jurisdiction over everyone within it.

If we do not want to die together in war, we must learn to live together in peace.
Harry S. Truman (1945)

Jaw, jaw is better than war, war.
Winston Churchill (c.1948)

It is essential, if man is not to be compelled to have recourse, as a last resort, to rebellion against tyranny and oppression, that human rights should be protected by the rule of law.
UN Declaration of Human Rights (1948)

■ explain common reasons for the breakdown of order among
nation-states, e.g., conflicts about national interests, ethnicity, and
religion; competition for resources and territory; the absence of
effective means to enforce international law

■ explain the consequences of the breakdown of order among
nation-states

■ explain why and how the breakdown of order among nation-states
can affect their own lives and the lives of others

3. **International organizations**. *Students should be able to evaluate,
    take, and defend positions on the purposes and functions of
    international organizations in the world today.*

    To achieve this standard, students should be able to

    ■ describe the purposes and functions of the major governmental
    international organizations, e.g., United Nations, NATO, World
    Court, Organization of American States

    ■ describe the purposes and functions of major nongovernmental
    international organizations, e.g., World Council of Churches, Roman
    Catholic Church, International Red Cross, Amnesty International,
    multinational corporations

*Human rights stand
upon a common basis;
and by all reason that
they are supported,
maintained, and
defended for all the
human family. The
essential
characteristics of
humanity are
everywhere the same.*

Frederick Douglass (1854)

B. **How do the domestic politics and constitutional
    principles of the United States affect its relations
    with the world?**

Content summary and rationale

At times in their history, Americans have sought to isolate themselves from
the rest of the world. At other times, the nation has played a prominent or
even dominant role in world affairs.

Domestic politics and the principles of the United States Constitution
impose constraints on the nation's relations with the rest of the world.
Disagreements over the meaning of these principles and the degree to which
they should guide the ends and means of foreign policy have raised some of
the most difficult issues in American history.

An understanding of the behavior of the United States in the world arena
and the processes by which foreign policy is made and implemented provides
the necessary foundation for making judgments about the proper direction
of American foreign policy.

Content standards

1. **The historical context of United States foreign policy.** *Students
    should be able to explain the principal foreign policy positions of the
    United States and evaluate their consequences.*

    To achieve this standard, students should be able to

    ■ explain the significance of principal policies and events in the United
    States' relations with the world, e.g., the American Revolution,
    Monroe Doctrine, Mexican and Spanish American Wars, World Wars
    I and II, formation of the United Nations, Marshall Plan, NATO,
    Korean and Vietnam Wars, end of the Cold War, interventions in Latin
    America

- explain how and why the United States assumed the role of world leader after World War II and what its leadership role is in the world today
- evaluate the major foreign policy positions that have characterized the United States' relations with the world, e.g., isolated nation, imperial power, and world leader

2. **Making and implementing United States foreign policy.** *Students should be able to evaluate, take, and defend positions about how United States foreign policy is made and the means by which it is carried out.*

To achieve this standard, students should be able to

- explain powers the Constitution gives to the president, Congress, and the federal judiciary in foreign affairs and how these powers have been used over time
- describe the process by which United States foreign policy is made, including the roles of federal agencies, domestic interest groups, the public, and the media
- explain the tension between constitutional provisions and the requirements of foreign policy, e.g., the power of Congress to declare war and the need for the president to make expeditious decisions in times of international emergency, the power of the president to make treaties and the need for the Senate to approve them
- describe the various means used to attain the ends of United States foreign policy, such as diplomacy; economic, military and humanitarian aid; treaties; sanctions; military intervention; covert action
- explain how and why domestic politics may impose constraints or obligations on the ways in which the United States acts in the world, e.g., long-standing commitments to certain nations, lobbying efforts of domestic groups, economic needs
- describe ways in which Americans can influence foreign policy

3. **The ends and means of United States foreign policy.** *Students should be able to evaluate, take, and defend positions on foreign policy issues in light of American national interests, values, and principles.*

To attain this standard, students should be able to

- explain the idea of the national interest
- evaluate the use of the national interest as a criterion for American foreign policy
- explain the influence of American constitutional values and principles on American foreign policy, e.g., a commitment to the self-determination of nations
- explain possible tensions among American values, principles, and interests as the nation deals with the practical requirements of international politics, e.g., a commitment to human rights and the requirements of national security
- evaluate the current role of the United States in peacemaking and peacekeeping

[P]eace, commerce, and honest friendship with all nations, entangling alliances with none....
Thomas Jefferson (1801)

Our policy [the Marshall Plan] is directed not against any country or doctrine but against hunger, poverty, desperation and chaos.
George C. Marshall (1947)

We must have a sense of unity and a national purpose in our foreign policy.
Ronald Reagan (1974)

C. How has the United States influenced other nations, and how have other nations influenced American politics and society?

Content summary and rationale

The United States does not exist in isolation; it is part of an interconnected world in whose development it has played and continues to play a considerable role. The American political tradition, including the ideas expressed in the Declaration of Independence, the United States Constitution, and the Bill of Rights, has had a profound influence abroad. The nation has exerted economic, technological, and cultural influence on other nations. At the same time, the United States and its citizens have been affected by political, economic, technological, and cultural influences from other countries.

Because of the interconnectedness of the world, many pressing domestic problems, including the economy and the environment, are also international issues. Thus, what once was considered a clear distinction between domestic and foreign policy is in some cases no longer valid.

To take part in debates about domestic and foreign policy, citizens need to be aware of developments in the world and their effects, and to evaluate proposals for dealing with them.

Content standards

1. **Impact of the American concept of democracy and individual rights on the world**. *Students should be able to evaluate, take, and defend positions about the impact of American political ideas on the world.*

    To achieve this standard, students should be able to

    ■ describe the impact on other nations of the American Revolution and of the values and principles expressed in the Declaration of Independence and the United States Constitution including the Bill of Rights

    ■ describe the influence abroad of American ideas about rights and how the ideas of others about rights have influenced Americans

2. **Political developments**. *Students should be able to evaluate, take, and defend positions about the effects of significant international political developments on the United States and other nations.*

    To achieve this standard, students should be able to

    ■ explain the effects on the United States of significant world political developments, e.g., the French, Russian, and Chinese Revolutions; rise of nationalism; World Wars I and II; decline of colonialism; terrorism; multiplication of nation-states and the proliferation of conflict within them; the emergence of regional organizations such as the European Union

---

Just what is it that America stands for? If she stands for one thing more than another, it is for the sovereignty of self-governing people.... She stands as an example of free institutions, and as an example of disinterested international action in the main tenets of justice.

Woodrow Wilson (1916)

What we call foreign affairs is no longer foreign affairs. It's a local affair. Whatever happens in Indonesia is important to Indiana....We cannot escape each other....

Dwight D. Eisenhower (1959)

- explain the effects on other nations of significant American political developments, e.g., immigration policies; opposition to communism; promotion of human rights; foreign trade; economic, military, and humanitarian aid

- explain why allegiance to some nation-states is being challenged by competing loyalties, such as those to ethnic, religious, tribal, or linguistic groups

- explain why transnational loyalties sometimes supersede loyalty to a nation-state, e.g., Communist International, Islam, Christianity

3. **Economic, technological, and cultural developments**. *Students should be able to evaluate, take, and defend positions about the effects of significant economic, technological, and cultural developments in the United States and other nations.*

   To achieve this standard, students should be able to

   - describe some of the principal economic, technological, and cultural effects the United States has had on the world, e.g., assembly line manufacturing, research and development in computer technology, popular music, fashion, film, television

   - explain the principal effects of developments in other nations on American society and on their own lives

     - economic conditions, e.g., multinational corporations, internationalization of capital, migration of labor, and other effects of an interdependent world economy

     - technological developments, e.g., fax machines, electronic communications networks, jet air travel, personal computers, television, motion pictures

     - cultural developments, e.g., religious movements, resurgence of ethnic consciousness, mass markets, sports

Economic, technological, and cultural developments in other nations have had significant effects on the United States.

4. **Demographic and environmental developments**. *Students should be able to evaluate, take, and defend positions about what the response of American governments at all levels should be to world demographic and environmental developments.*

   To achieve this standard, students should be able to

   - describe the impact of major demographic trends on the United States, e.g., population growth, immigration

   - describe principal environmental conditions that affect the United States, e.g., destruction of rain forests, air pollution, water pollution

   - evaluate historical and contemporary responses of the American government to demographic and environmental changes

5. **United States and international organizations**. *Students should be able to evaluate, take, and defend positions about what the relationship of the United States should be to international organizations.*

To achieve this standard, students should be able to

■ describe the role of the United States in establishing and maintaining principal international organizations, e.g., UN, UNICEF, GATT, World Bank, NATO, OAS, International Monetary Fund

■ identify some important bilateral and multilateral agreements to which the United States is signatory, e.g., NAFTA, Helsinki Accord, Antarctic Treaty, Most Favored Nation Agreements

■ evaluate the role of the United States in international organizations

V. WHAT ARE THE ROLES OF THE CITIZEN IN AMERICAN DEMOCRACY?

A. What is citizenship?

Content summary and rationale

Citizenship in American constitutional democracy differs from membership in an authoritarian or totalitarian regime. In American democracy each citizen is a full and equal member of a self-governing community endowed with fundamental rights and entrusted with responsibilities.

Both the government and the citizens are responsible for the protection of the rights of individuals and for the promotion of the common good. It is a fundamental responsibility of the citizen to see that government serves the purposes for which it was created.

In order to fulfill this role, individuals need to understand what citizenship means in American constitutional democracy.

Content standards

1. **The meaning of citizenship in the United States**. *Students should be able to explain the meaning of citizenship in the United States.*

   To achieve this standard, students should be able to

   ■ explain the idea that citizenship

     ▪ is legally recognized membership in a self-governing community

     ▪ confers full membership in a self-governing community; no degrees of citizenship or legally recognized states of inferior citizenship are tolerated

     ▪ confers equal rights under the law

     ▪ is not dependent on inherited, involuntary groupings such as race, ethnicity, or ancestral religion

     ▪ confers certain rights and privileges, e.g., the right to vote, to hold public office, to serve on juries

   ■ explain that Americans are citizens of both their state and the United States

2. **Becoming a citizen**. *Students should be able to evaluate, take, and defend positions on issues regarding the criteria used for naturalization.*

   ■ explain the distinction between citizens and noncitizens (aliens) and the process by which aliens may become citizens

   ■ compare naturalization in the United States with that of other nations

   ■ evaluate the criteria used for admission to citizenship in the United States:

     ▪ residence in the United States for five years

In view of the Constitution, in the eye of the law, there is in this country no superior, dominant, ruling class of citizens. There is no caste here. Our Constitution is color-blind, and neither knows nor tolerates classes among citizens. In respect of civil rights, all citizens are equal before the law. The humblest is the peer of the most powerful.

John Marshall Harlan (1896)

[T]he only title in our democracy superior to that of President [is] the title of citizen.

Louis Brandeis (c.1937)

Center for Civic Education

- ability to read, write, and speak English
- proof of good moral character
- knowledge of the history of the United States
- knowledge of and support for the values and principles of American constitutional government

B. What are the rights of citizens?

Content summary and rationale

In a political system in which one of the primary purposes of government is the protection of individual rights, it is important for citizens to understand what these rights are and their relationship to each other and to other values and interests of their society.

The concept of rights is complex and cannot be treated thoroughly in this set of standards. These standards, however, will provide a basis for the analysis of public issues involving rights. To do so, it is useful to distinguish among three categories of rights that are of particular significance in the American political system. These are personal, political, and economic rights.

Few rights, if any, are considered absolute. Rights may reinforce or conflict with each other or with other values and interests and require reasonable limitations. Therefore, it is important for citizens to develop a framework that clarifies their ideas about rights and the relationships among rights and other values and interests. This framework provides a basis for making reasoned decisions about the proper scope and limits of rights.

Content standards

1. **Personal rights**. *Students should be able to evaluate, take, and defend positions on issues regarding personal rights.*

    To achieve this standard, students should be able to

    - explain the meaning of personal rights as distinguished from political rights, e.g., the right to privacy or the right to freedom of conscience as distinguished from the political right to peaceably assemble and petition for a redress of grievances
    - identify major documentary statements of personal rights, e.g., the Declaration of Independence, the Northwest Ordinance, the United States Constitution including the Bill of Rights, state constitutions and bills of rights
    - explain the importance to the individual and to society of such personal rights as
        - freedom of thought and conscience
        - privacy and personal autonomy
        - freedom of expression and association
        - freedom of movement and residence
        - right to due process of law and equal protection of the law

There is no security for the personal or political rights of any man in a community where any man is deprived of his personal or political rights.

Benjamin Harrison (1892)

The house of everyone is to him as his castle and fortress, as well for his defense against injury and violence as for his repose.

Sir Edward Coke (c.1620)

- explain how personal rights are secured in American constitutional democracy by such means as the rule of law, checks and balances, an independent judiciary, a vigilant citizenry

- evaluate contemporary issues that involve the question of personal rights, e.g., restricted membership in organizations, school prayer, sexual harassment, refusal of medical care

2. **Political rights**. *Students should be able to evaluate, take, and defend positions on issues regarding political rights.*

To achieve this standard, students should be able to

- explain the meaning of political rights as distinguished from personal rights, e.g., the right of free speech for political discussion as distinct from the right of free speech for expression of one's personal tastes and interests, or the right to register to vote as distinct from the right to live where one chooses

- identify the major documentary statements of political rights—the Declaration of Independence, the Northwest Ordinance, the United States Constitution including the Bill of Rights, state constitutions and bills of rights, civil rights legislation, court decisions

- explain the importance to the individual and society of such political rights as

    - freedom of speech, press, assembly, petition

    - right to vote and run for public office

- explain how political rights are secured by constitutional government and by such means as the rule of law, checks and balances, an independent judiciary, and a vigilant citizenry

- evaluate contemporary issues that involve political rights, e.g., proportional voting, "hate speech," access to classified information, changing the boundaries of congressional and state legislative districts

3. **Economic rights**. *Students should be able to evaluate, take, and defend positions on issues regarding economic rights.*

To achieve this standard, students should be able to

- explain the meaning of economic rights as distinguished from personal and political rights, e.g., the right to use money to buy personal property as distinct from the right to donate money for political campaigns

- identify major documentary statements of economic rights—the Declaration of Independence, the United States Constitution including the Bill of Rights, state constitutions and bills of rights, legislation, court decisions, and the common law

- explain the importance to the individual and society of such economic rights as the right to

    - acquire, use, transfer, and dispose of property

    - choose one's work, change employment

    - join labor unions and professional associations

Congress shall make no law respecting an establishment of religion, or prohibiting the free exercise thereof; or abridging the freedom of speech, or of the press, or the right of the people peaceably to assemble, and to petition the Government for a redress of grievances.
First Amendment (1791)

I believe each individual is naturally entitled to do as he pleases with himself and the fruit of his labor, so far as it in no wise interferes with any other man's rights.
Abraham Lincoln (1858)

Center for Civic Education

- establish and operate a business
- copyright and patent
- enter into lawful contracts
- explain how economic rights are secured by constitutional government and by such means as the rule of law, checks and balances, an independent judiciary, and a vigilant citizenry
- evaluate the view that economic responsibilities follow from economic rights
- evaluate contemporary issues that involve economic rights, e.g., minimum wages, consumer product safety, taxation, affirmative action, eminent domain, zoning, copyright, patents

We must preserve the right of free speech and the right of free assembly. But the right of free speech does not carry with it—as has been said—the right to holler fire in a crowded theatre. We must preserve the right to free assembly. But free assembly does not carry with it the right to block public thoroughfares to traffic. We do have a right to protest. And a right to march under conditions that do not infringe the Constitutional rights of our neighbors.

Lyndon B. Johnson (1965)

4. **Relationships among personal, political, and economic rights.** *Students should be able to evaluate, take, and defend positions on the relationships among personal, political, and economic rights.*

To achieve this standard, students should be able to

- explain the relationship between the economic right to acquire, use, transfer, and dispose of property to political rights
- explain the relationship of economic rights such as the right to choose one's work, to change employment, and to join a labor union and other lawful associations to political rights
- explain and give examples of situations in which personal, political, or economic rights are in conflict
- evaluate the argument that poverty, unemployment, and urban decay serve to limit both political and economic rights
- evaluate the argument that personal, political, and economic rights reinforce each other

5. **Scope and limits of rights.** *Students should be able to evaluate, take, and defend positions on issues regarding the proper scope and limits of rights.*

To achieve this standard, students should be able to

- explain what is meant by the "scope and limits" of a right, e.g., the scope of one's right to free speech in the United States is extensive and protects almost all forms of political expression; however, the right to free speech can be limited if and when speech seriously harms or endangers others
- evaluate the argument that all rights have limits
- explain considerations and criteria commonly used in determining what limits should be placed on specific rights, e.g.,
  - clear and present danger
  - compelling government interest
  - national security
  - chilling effect on the exercise of rights
  - libel or slander

- public safety
- equal opportunity
- evaluate positions on contemporary conflicts between rights, e.g., the right to a fair trial and the right to a free press, the right to privacy and the right to freedom of expression, one person's right to free speech versus another's right to be heard
- evaluate positions on a contemporary conflict between rights and other social values and interests, e.g., the right of the public to know what their government is doing versus the need for national security, the right to property versus the protection of the environment

C. What are the responsibilities of citizens?

Content summary and rationale

The purposes of American constitutional democracy are furthered by citizens who continuously reexamine the basic principles of the Constitution and monitor the performance of political leaders and government agencies to insure their fidelity to constitutional values and principles. In addition, they must examine their own behavior and fidelity to these values and principles.

Citizens also need to examine situations in which their responsibilities may require that their personal desires or interests be subordinated to the common good. To make these judgments requires an understanding of the difference between personal and civic responsibilities as well as the mutual reinforcement of these responsibilities.

Content standards

1. **Personal responsibilities**. *Students should be able to evaluate, take, and defend positions on issues regarding the personal responsibilities of citizens in American constitutional democracy.*

   To achieve this standard, students should be able to

   - explain the distinction between personal and civic responsibilities, as well as the tensions that may arise between them
   - evaluate the importance for the individual and society of
     - taking care of one's self
     - supporting one's family and caring for, nurturing, and educating one's children
     - accepting responsibility for the consequences of one's actions
     - adhering to moral principles
     - considering the rights and interests of others
     - behaving in a civil manner

The only thing necessary for the triumph of evil is for good men to do nothing.
Edmund Burke (c.1780)

In Germany the Nazis came first for the Communists, and I didn't speak up because I wasn't a Communist. Then they came for the Jews, and I didn't speak up because I wasn't a Jew. Then they came for the trade unionists, and I didn't speak up because I wasn't a trade unionist. Then they came for the Catholics, and I didn't speak up because I was a Protestant. Then they came for me, and by that time no one was left to speak up.
Attributed to Martin Niemoeller (1892-1984)

No government action, no economic doctrine, no economic plan or project can replace that God-imposed responsibility of the individual man and woman to their neighbors.
Herbert Hoover (1931)

2. **Civic responsibilities.** *Students should be able to evaluate, take, and defend positions on issues regarding civic responsibilities of citizens in American constitutional democracy.*

To achieve this standard, students should be able to

■ evaluate the importance of each citizen reflecting on, criticizing, and reaffirming basic constitutional principles

■ evaluate the importance for the individual and society of

   ■ obeying the law

   ■ being informed and attentive to public issues

   ■ monitoring the adherence of political leaders and governmental agencies to constitutional principles and taking appropriate action if that adherence is lacking

   ■ assuming leadership when appropriate

   ■ paying taxes

   ■ registering to vote and voting knowledgeably on candidates and issues

   ■ serving as a juror

   ■ serving in the armed forces

   ■ performing public service

■ evaluate whether and when their obligations as citizens require that their personal desires and interests be subordinated to the public good

■ evaluate whether and when moral obligations or constitutional principles require one to refuse to assume certain civic responsibilities

D. What civic dispositions or traits of private and public character are important to the preservation and improvement of American constitutional democracy?

Content summary and rationale

American constitutional democracy requires the responsible self-governance of each individual; one cannot exist without the other. Traits of private character such as moral responsibility, self-discipline, and respect for individual worth and human dignity are essential to its well-being.

American constitutional democracy cannot accomplish its purposes, however, unless its citizens are inclined to participate thoughtfully in public affairs. Traits of public character such as public spiritedness, civility, respect for law, critical mindedness, and a willingness to negotiate and compromise are indispensable for its vitality.

These traits of private and public character also contribute to the political efficacy of the individual, the healthy functioning of the political system, and the individual's sense of dignity and worth.

Content standards

1. **Dispositions that lead the citizen to be an independent member of society.** *Students should be able to evaluate, take, and defend positions on the importance to American constitutional democracy of dispositions that lead individuals to become independent members of society.*

    To achieve this standard, students should be able to

    ■ explain the meaning and importance of self-discipline and self-governance—adhering voluntarily to self-imposed standards of behavior rather than requiring the imposition of external controls

    ■ explain the meaning and importance of individual responsibility— fulfilling the moral and legal obligations of membership in society

2. **Dispositions that foster respect for individual worth and human dignity.** *Students should be able to evaluate, take, and defend positions on the importance to American constitutional democracy of dispositions that foster respect for individual worth and human dignity.*

    To achieve this standard, students should be able to

    ■ explain the meaning and importance of respect for the rights and choices of individuals—even beyond the legally enforceable rights guaranteed by the Constitution—such as holding and advocating differing ideas and joining associations to advance their views

    ■ explain the meaning and importance of compassion—concern for the well-being of others

3. **Dispositions that incline the citizen to public affairs.** *Students should be able to evaluate, take, and defend positions on the importance to American constitutional democracy of dispositions that incline citizens to public affairs.*

    To achieve this standard, students should be able to

    ■ explain the meaning of civic mindedness—what the Founders called civic virtue—or attentiveness to and concern for public affairs

    ■ explain the meaning of patriotism—loyalty to the values and principles underlying American constitutional democracy as distinguished from jingoism and chauvinism

4. **Dispositions that facilitate thoughtful and effective participation in public affairs.** *Students should be able to evaluate, take, and defend positions on the importance to American constitutional democracy of dispositions that facilitate thoughtful and effective participation in public affairs.*

    To achieve this standard, students should be able to

    ■ evaluate the usefulness of the following traits in facilitating thoughtful and effective participation in public affairs

Active citizens...are public meeting-goers and joiners of voluntary organizations who discuss and deliberate with others about the policies that will affect them all, and who serve their country not only as taxpayers and occasional soldiers, but by having a considered notion of the public good that they genuinely take to heart. The good citizen is a patriot.
Judith Shklar (1991)

Civility costs nothing and buys everything.
Lady Mary Wortley Montagu (1756)

The life of the nation is secure only while the nation is honest, truthful, and virtuous.
Frederick Douglass (1885)

Center for Civic Education

Some people look upon any setback as the end. They're always looking for the benediction rather than the invocation....But you can't quit. That isn't the way our country was built.

**Hubert H. Humphrey
(c.1968)**

No man is an island, entire of itself; every man is a piece of the continent, a part of the main; if a clod be washed away by the sea, Europe is the less, as well as if a promontory were, as well as if a manor of thy friend's or of thine own were; any man's death diminishes me, because I am involved in mankind; and therefore never send to know for whom the bell tolls; it tolls for thee.

John Donne (1631)

Whether in private or in public, the good citizen does something to support democratic habits and the constitutional order.

Judith Shklar (1991)

- **civility**—treating other persons respectfully, regardless of whether or not one agrees with their viewpoints; being willing to listen to other points of view; avoiding hostile, abusive, emotional, and illogical argument

- **respect for the rights of other individuals**—having respect for others' right to an equal voice in government, to be equal in the eyes of the law, to hold and advocate diverse ideas, and to join in associations to advance their views

- **respect for law**—willingness to abide by laws, even though one may not be in complete agreement with every law; willingness to work through peaceful, legal means to change laws which one thinks to be unwise or unjust

- **honesty**—willingness to seek and express the truth

- **open mindedness**—considering others' points of view

- **critical mindedness**—having the inclination to question the validity of various positions, including one's own

- **negotiation and compromise**—making an effort to come to agreement with those with whom one may differ, when it is reasonable and morally justifiable to do so

- **persistence**—being willing to attempt again and again to accomplish worthwhile goals

- **civic mindedness**—paying attention to and having concern for public affairs

- **compassion**—having concern for the well-being of others, especially for the less fortunate

- **patriotism**—being loyal to the values and principles underlying American constitutional democracy, as distinguished from jingoism and chauvinism

- **courage**—the strength to stand up for one's convictions, when conscience demands

- **tolerance of ambiguity**—the ability to accept uncertainties that arise, e.g., from insufficient knowledge or understanding of complex issues or from tension among fundamental values and principles

E. How can citizens take part in civic life?

The well-being of American constitutional democracy depends upon the informed and effective participation of citizens concerned with the preservation of individual rights and the promotion of the common good. The strength and significance of Americans' participatory habits were remarked upon in the nineteenth century by Alexis de Tocqueville, who was struck by the degree of their social participation. Americans have retained this characteristic of engaging in cooperative action for common purposes. Participation in political life, contrasted with the wider realm of organized social participation, has ebbed in recent decades, however. Indifference to or alienation from politics may characterize a significant segment of the population. Citizens should realize that their intelligence and energy are needed in political forums, that democracy wanes when citizens shun politics.

There are two general ways to approach problems that confront society. One is through social action; the other is through political action. For example, in dealing with crime, a course of social action might include forming a neighborhood watch. A course of political action might include meeting with officials, demanding that police provide adequate protection, and agreeing to pay the necessary taxes for them to do so. In dealing with hunger, social action might include working in a soup kitchen organized by a charitable organization; political action might include devising a government program to feed the hungry and acting to insure its adoption and public funding.

Social and political action are not mutually exclusive; they may overlap. In given circumstances, however, one approach may be more appropriate. Both political and social action are essential for the health of American constitutional democracy.

If citizens want their voices to be heard, they must become active participants in the political process. Although elections, campaigns, and voting are at the center of democratic institutions, citizens should be aware that beyond electoral politics there is a wide range of participatory opportunities available to them. These possibilities include attending political meetings, contacting public officials, joining advocacy groups and political parties, and taking part in demonstrations.

Political leadership and careers in public service are vitally important in a democratic society. Citizens need to understand the contributions of those in public service as well as the practical and ethical dilemmas political leaders face.

To answer the question "Why should I participate in the political system?" the citizen needs to examine and evaluate the relationships between the attainment of individual and public goals on one hand and participation in the life of the political community on the other.

If American constitutional democracy is to endure, its citizens must recognize that it is not "a machine that would go of itself." They also must be aware of the difficulty of establishing free institutions, as evidenced by the experience of the Founders as well as events in the contemporary world. American constitutional democracy requires the continuing and dedicated participation of an attentive, knowledgeable, and reflective citizenry.

> *Inside the polling booth every American man and woman stands as the equal of every other American man and woman. There they have no superiors. There they have no masters save their own minds and consciences.*
> **Franklin Delano Roosevelt** (1936)

> *As citizens of this democracy, you are the rulers and the ruled, the lawgivers and the law-abiding, the beginning and the end.*
> **Adlai Stevenson (c.1956)**

> *Where everyman is...participator in the government of affairs, not merely at an election one day in the year but every day...he will let the heart be torn out of his body sooner than his power be wrested from him by a Caesar or a Bonaparte.*
> **Thomas Jefferson (1816)**

Content standards

1. **The relationship between politics and the attainment of individual and public goals**. *Students should be able to evaluate, take and defend positions on the relationship between politics and the attainment of individual and public goals.*

   To achieve this standard, students should be able to

   - explain the relationship of individual participation in the political process to the realization of the fundamental values of American constitutional democracy
   - explain the relationship between participation in the political process and the attainment of individual and collective goals

2. The difference between political and social participation. *Students should be able to explain the difference between political and social participation.*

To achieve this standard, students should be able to

■ explain what distinguishes participation in government and political life from nonpolitical participation in civil society and private life, e.g., participating in a campaign to change laws regulating nursing homes as opposed to volunteering to work in a nursing home

■ evaluate the importance of both political and social participation to American constitutional democracy

3. Forms of political participation. *Students should be able to evaluate, take, and defend positions about the means that citizens should use to monitor and influence the formation and implementation of public policy.*

To achieve this standard, students should be able to

■ describe the many ways citizens can participate in the political process at local, state, and national levels

■ describe historical and current examples of citizen movements seeking to expand liberty, to insure the equal rights of all citizens, and/or to realize other values fundamental to American constitutional democracy, such as the suffrage and civil rights movements

■ explain what civil disobedience is, how it differs from other forms of protest, what its consequences might be, and evaluate the circumstances under which it might be justified

■ evaluate the importance of voting as a form of political participation

■ evaluate the usefulness of other forms of political participation in influencing public policy, e.g., attending political and governmental meetings, filing a legal challenge, demonstrating, contacting public officials, working in campaigns, contributing money to political parties or causes, writing letters, boycotting, community organizing, petitioning, picketing, expressing opinions on talk shows, running for political office

4. Political leadership and careers in public service. *Students should be able to evaluate, take, and defend positions about the functions of leadership in a American constitutional democracy.*

To achieve this standard, students should be able to

■ explain the functions of political leadership and why leadership is a vital necessity in American constitutional democracy

■ describe various ways one can exercise leadership in public affairs

■ describe opportunities for citizens to engage in careers in public service

■ describe the personal qualities necessary for political leadership

■ explain and evaluate ethical dilemmas that might confront political leaders

5. Knowledge and participation. *Students should be able to explain the importance of knowledge to competent and responsible participation in American democracy.*

To achieve this standard, students should be able to

- explain why becoming knowledgeable about public affairs and the values and principles of American constitutional democracy and communicating that knowledge to others is an important form of participation

- explain how awareness of the nature of American constitutional democracy may give citizens the ability to reaffirm or change fundamental constitutional values

- evaluate the claim that constitutional democracy requires the participation of an attentive, knowledgeable, and competent citizenry

In a time of turbulence and change, it is more true than ever that knowledge is power.
John F. Kennedy (1962)

No free government, nor the blessings of liberty, can be preserved to any people, but by...a frequent recurrence to fundamental principles.
George Mason (1776)

Appendices

ORGANIZING QUESTIONS AND CONTENT SUMMARY
PART I

K - 4	5 - 8	9 - 12
I. WHAT IS GOVERNMENT AND WHAT SHOULD IT DO?	**I. WHAT ARE CIVIC LIFE, POLITICS, AND GOVERNMENT?**	**I. WHAT ARE CIVIC LIFE, POLITICS, AND GOVERNMENT?**
Defining government	Defining civic life, politics, and government	Defining civic life, politics, and government
Defining power and authority	Necessity and purposes of government	Necessity of politics and government
Necessity and purposes of government	Limited and unlimited governments	The purposes of politics and government
Functions of government	The rule of law	Limited and unlimited governments
Purposes of rules and laws	Concepts of "constitution"	The rule of law
Evaluating rules and laws	Purposes and uses of constitutions	Civil society and government
Limited and unlimited governments	Conditions under which constitutional government flourishes	The relationship of limited government to political and economic freedom
Importance of limited government	Shared powers and parliamentary systems	Concepts of "constitution"
	Confederal, federal, and unitary systems	Purposes and uses of constitutions
		Conditions under which constitutional government flourishes
		Shared powers and parliamentary systems
		Confederal, federal, and unitary systems
		Nature of representation

Center for Civic Education

ORGANIZING QUESTIONS AND CONTENT SUMMARY
PART II

K - 4	5 - 8	9 - 12
II. WHAT ARE THE BASIC VALUES AND PRINCIPLES OF AMERICAN DEMOCRACY?	**II. WHAT ARE THE FOUNDATIONS OF THE AMERICAN POLITICAL SYSTEM?**	**II. WHAT ARE THE FOUNDATIONS OF THE AMERICAN POLITICAL SYSTEM?**
Fundamental values and principles	The American idea of constitutional government	The American idea of constitutional government
Distinctive characteristics of American society	Distinctive characteristics of American society	How American constitutional government has shaped the character of American society
American identity	The role of voluntarism in American life	Distinctive characteristics of American society
Diversity in American society	Diversity in American society	The role of voluntarism in American life
Prevention and management of conflicts	American identity	The role of organized groups in political life
Promoting ideals	The character of American political conflict	Diversity in American society
	Fundamental values and principles	American national identity and political culture
	Conflicts among values and principles in American political and social life	Character of American political conflict
	Disparities between ideals and reality in American political and social life	Liberalism and American constitutional democracy
		Republicanism and American constitutional democracy
		Fundamental values and principles
		Conflicts among values and principles in American political and social life
		Disparities between ideals and reality in American political and social life

ORGANIZING QUESTIONS AND CONTENT SUMMARY
PART III

K - 4	5 - 8	9 - 12
III. HOW DOES THE GOVERNMENT ESTABLISHED BY THE CONSTITUTION EMBODY THE PURPOSES, VALUES, AND PRINCIPLES OF AMERICAN DEMOCRACY? The meaning and importance of the United States Constitution Organization and major responsibilities of the national government Organization and major responsibilities of state governments Organization and major responsibilities of local governments Identifying members of government	**III. HOW DOES THE GOVERNMENT ESTABLISHED BY THE CONSTITUTION EMBODY THE PURPOSES, VALUES, AND PRINCIPLES OF AMERICAN DEMOCRACY?** Distributing, sharing, and limiting powers of the national government Sharing of powers between the national and state governments Major responsibilities for domestic and foreign policy Financing government through taxation State governments Organization and responsibilities of state and local governments Who represents you in legislative and executive branches of your local, state, and national governments The place of law in American society Criteria for evaluating rules and laws Judicial protection of the rights of individuals The public agenda Political communication Political parties, campaigns, and elections Associations and groups Forming and carrying out public policy	**III. HOW DOES THE GOVERNMENT ESTABLISHED BY THE CONSTITUTION EMBODY THE PURPOSES, VALUES, AND PRINCIPLES OF AMERICAN DEMOCRACY?** Distributing governmental power and preventing its abuse The American federal system The institutions of the national government Major responsibilities of the national government in domestic and foreign policy Financing government through taxation The constitutional status of state and local governments Organization of state and local governments Major responsibilities of state and local governments The place of law in American society Judicial protection of the rights of individuals The public agenda Public opinion and behavior of the electorate Political communication: television, radio, the press, and political persuasion Political parties, campaigns, and elections Associations and groups Forming and carrying out public policy

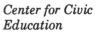

Center for Civic Education

ORGANIZING QUESTIONS AND CONTENT SUMMARY
PART IV

K - 4	5 - 8	9 - 12
IV. WHAT IS THE RELATIONSHIP OF THE UNITED STATES TO OTHER NATIONS AND TO WORLD AFFAIRS? Nations Interaction among nations	**IV. WHAT IS THE RELATIONSHIP OF THE UNITED STATES TO OTHER NATIONS AND TO WORLD AFFAIRS?** Nation-states Interaction among nation-states United States' relations with other nation-states International organizations Impact of the American concept of democracy and individual rights on the world Political, demographic, and environmental developments	**IV. WHAT IS THE RELATIONSHIP OF THE UNITED STATES TO OTHER NATIONS AND TO WORLD AFFAIRS?** Nation-states Interactions among nation-states International organizations The historical context of United States foreign policy Making and implementing United States foreign policy The ends and means of United States foreign policy Impact of the American concept of democracy and individual rights on the world Political developments Economic, technological, and cultural developments Demographic and environmental developments United States and international organizations

ORGANIZING QUESTIONS AND CONTENT SUMMARY
PART V

K - 4	5 - 8	9 - 12
V. WHAT ARE THE ROLES OF THE CITIZEN IN AMERICAN DEMOCRACY?	**V. WHAT ARE THE ROLES OF THE CITIZEN IN AMERICAN DEMOCRACY?**	**V. WHAT ARE THE ROLES OF THE CITIZEN IN AMERICAN DEMOCRACY?**
The meaning of citizenship	The meaning of citizenship	The meaning of citizenship in the United States
Becoming a citizen	Becoming a citizen	Becoming a citizen
Rights of individuals	Personal rights	Personal rights
Responsibilities of individuals	Political rights	Political rights
Dispositions that enhance citizen effectiveness and promote the healthy functioning of American democracy	Economic rights	Economic rights
Forms of participation	Scope and limits of rights	Relationships among personal, political, and economic rights
Political leadership and public service	Personal responsibilities	Scope and limits of rights
Selecting leaders	Civic responsibilities	Personal responsibilities
	Dispositions that enhance citizen effectiveness and promote the healthy functioning of American constitutional democracy	Civic responsibilities
	Participation in civic and political life and the attainment of individual and public goals	Dispositions that lead the citizen to be an independent member of society
	The difference between political and social participation	Dispositions that foster respect for individual worth and human dignity
	Forms of political participation	Dispositions that incline the citizen to public affairs
	Political leadership and public service	Dispositions that facilitate thoughtful and effective participation in public affairs
	Knowledge and participation	The relationship between politics and the attainment of individual and public goals
		The difference between political and social participation
		Forms of political participation
		Political leadership and careers in public service
		Knowledge and participation

Center for Civic Education

ILLUSTRATIVE PERFORMANCE STANDARD

Performance standards are statements of criteria for determining desirable levels of achievement of content standards. They specify "how good is good enough."

Students can demonstrate their achievement of content standards in various ways, such as:

- **written performances**, including short answer, multiple choice, and essay examinations; research papers
- **oral performances**, including oral reports, participation in simulated public hearings, mock trial and appellate court proceedings, panel discussions, and debates
- **participatory activities**, including serving as participant/leader in committee meetings, panel discussions, student government, student courts, and civic organizations
- **visual and audio presentations**, including charts, graphs, diagrams, models, portfolios, video and audio tapes

Regardless of the means (e.g., written essay, oral presentation) chosen to demonstrate achievement of a content standard, students' responses should give evidence that they have understood major concepts, know relevant historical and contemporary conditions and developments, and, where applicable, can use what they have learned to evaluate, take, and defend positions on current issues.

The performance standard that follows is presented to illustrate what performance standards are and how they relate to content standards. These performance standards will specify appropriate levels of increasingly sophisticated student responses, each building on the previous response. For example, in the following illustrative performance standard from grades 9-12, the

- **basic level** provides criteria to determine if students can explain the essential characteristics of limited and unlimited governments and identify at least one historical and contemporary example of such governments
- **proficient level** provides criteria to determine if, in addition to satisfying the basic level, students can explain the differences between such forms of limited governments as constitutional democracies and such forms of unlimited governments as authoritarian and totalitarian systems
- **advanced level** provides criteria to determine if, in addition to satisfying criteria for the basic and proficient levels, students can demonstrate a deeper understanding of the characteristics of these types of governments including, for example, the role of civil society in limited and unlimited governments and the role of ideology in authoritarian and totalitarian regimes

Illustrative Performance Standard (9-12)

Content standard

1. **Limited and unlimited governments**. *Students should be able to explain the essential characteristics of limited and unlimited governments.*

    To achieve this standard students should be able to

    - describe the essential characteristics of limited and unlimited governments
        - limited governments have established and respected restraints on their power, e.g.,
            - constitutional government—governments characterized by legal limits on political power
        - unlimited governments are those in which there are no regularized and effective means of restraining their power, i.e.,
            - authoritarian systems—governments in which political power is concentrated in one person or a small group, and individuals and groups are subordinated to that power
            - totalitarian systems—modern forms of extreme authoritarianism in which the government attempts to control every aspect of the lives of individuals and prohibits independent associations
    - identify historical and contemporary examples of limited and unlimited governments and explain their classification, e.g.,
        - limited governments—United States, Great Britain, Botswana, Japan, Israel, Chile
        - unlimited governments—Nazi Germany, Imperial Japan, Spain under Franco, Argentina under Peron, Iraq under Hussein, Iran

Performance standard

BASIC LEVEL—To demonstrate a **basic** level of proficiency, a student's response should include the following major characteristics of limited and unlimited government and provide at least one historical and contemporary example of each type of government.

LIMITED GOVERNMENTS	UNLIMITED GOVERNMENTS
MAJOR CHARACTERISTICS	
Constitutional governments	**Non-constitutional governments**
<ul><li>powers effectively restricted by constitutions and other laws, e.g.,<ul><li>goals of government and means used to attain them do not violate the constitution</li><li>effective limits on police/court powers</li><li>limits on powers of executive and legislatures</li><li>laws apply to governors as well as the governed</li></ul></li></ul>	<ul><li>constitutional restraints, if any, not effective e.g.,<ul><li>police power not effectively limited</li><li>courts controlled by executive</li><li>executive not restricted by a legislature or the courts</li></ul></li></ul>
HISTORICAL EXAMPLES	
<ul><li>the United States</li><li>Great Britain</li></ul>	<ul><li>Italy under Mussolini</li><li>Spain under Franco</li></ul>
CONTEMPORARY EXAMPLES	
<ul><li>Israel</li><li>Japan</li></ul>	<ul><li>Iraq</li><li>Libya</li></ul>

PROFICIENT LEVEL—To demonstrate a **proficient** level of performance, a student's response should include the basic characteristics and the following additional characteristics of limited and unlimited governments.

LIMITED GOVERNMENTS	UNLIMITED GOVERNMENTS
MAJOR CHARACTERISTICS	
Constitutional governments	**Non-constitutional governments**
■ institutional devices used to limit powers, e.g., 　■ written or unwritten constitutions 　■ independent judiciaries 　■ checks and balances 　■ separation of powers 　■ bill of rights 　■ regular, free, and fair elections ■ powers are limited to the purposes specified in a constitution, e.g., the protection of individual rights and promotion of the common good	**Authoritarian systems** ■ unlimited authority exercised by an individual or group ■ individual rights subordinated to state ■ no regularized and effective restraints on powers of government, e.g., 　■ no popularly elected assembly 　■ no free elections 　■ no independent judiciary **Totalitarian systems** ■ government attempts to control every aspect of the lives of individuals and prohibits independent associations ■ government use of intimidation and terror
HISTORICAL EXAMPLES	
■ Canada ■ Australia ■ New Zealand ■ United States	**Authoritarian systems** ■ Russia under the Czars ■ Japan under the military in the 1930s **Totalitarian systems** ■ Soviet Union under Stalin ■ Germany under Hitler ■ China under Mao ■ Romania under Ceausescu ■ Cambodia under Pol Pot ■ North Korea under Kim-Il-sung
CONTEMPORARY EXAMPLES	
■ Botswana ■ Japan ■ Denmark ■ Venezuela ■ United States	**Authoritarian systems** ■ Kenya ■ Myanmar (Burma) **Totalitarian systems** ■ Cuba under Castro ■ Iraq under Saddam Hussein

ADVANCED LEVEL—To demonstrate an **advanced** level of performance, a student's response should include the basic and proficient characteristics and the following additional characteristics of limited and unlimited governments.

LIMITED GOVERNMENTS	UNLIMITED GOVERNMENTS
MAJOR CHARACTERISTICS	
Constitutional governments	**Non-constitutional governments**
■ provide protection of a private sphere of life free from unreasonable interference from government ■ active presence of more than one political party; concept of "loyal opposition" ■ active presence of civil society composed of numerous nongovernmental organizations and groups	**Authoritarian systems** ■ often military or quasi-military in character ■ often nationalistic/fundamentalist ■ ban organizations deemed to be a threat ■ civil society restricted in accordance with the interests of the regime **Totalitarian systems** ■ ideology as a secular religion ■ control of education, literature, the arts, religion, and mass communication ■ control or bans on travel and emigration ■ a few centers of power/influence outside the ruling party (e.g., armed forces, scientific elite) may be permitted ■ civil society non-existent, because independent organizations and associations are not allowed

GLOSSARY

affirmative action. Policy or program designed to redress historic injustices committed against racial minorities and other specified groups by making special efforts to provide members of these groups with access to educational and employment opportunities.

alien. Anyone not a citizen of the country in which he or she lives.

amendment (constitutional). Changes in, or additions to, a constitution. Proposed by a two-thirds vote of both houses of Congress or by a convention called by Congress at the request of two-thirds of the state legislatures. Ratified by approval of three-fourths of the states.

anarchy. Absence of formal legal order; also the social context in which legitimate political authority does not exist.

Articles of Confederation. First constitution of the United States, 1781. Created a weak national government, replaced in 1789 by the Constitution of the United States.

authority. Right to control or direct the actions of others, legitimized by law, morality, custom, or consent.

Bill of Rights. First ten amendments to the Constitution. Ratified in 1791, these amendments limit governmental power and protect basic rights and liberties of individuals.

Bill of Rights of 1689. See *English Bill of Rights*.

British constitution. Framework for running the British government. The British constitution is unwritten, consisting of common law, acts of Parliament, and political customs and traditions.

Brown v. Board of Education (1954). Supreme Court case which declared that "separate-but-equal" educational facilities are inherently unequal and therefore a violation of equal protection of the law guaranteed by the Fourteenth Amendment.

bureaucracy. Organizations that implement government policies.

cabinet. Secretaries, or chief administrators, of the major departments of the federal government. Cabinet secretaries are appointed by the president with the consent of the Senate.

caste system. Divisions in society based on differences of wealth, inherited rank, privilege, profession, or occupation.

chauvinism. Fanatical patriotism, blind devotion to and belief in the superiority of one's group.

checks and balances. Constitutional mechanisms that authorize each branch of government to share powers with the other branches and thereby check their activities. For example, the president may veto legislation passed by Congress, the Senate must confirm major executive appointments, and the courts may declare acts of Congress unconstitutional.

citizen. Member of a political society who therefore owes allegiance to and is entitled to protection by and from the government.

citizenship. Status of being a member of a state, one who owes allegiance to the government and is entitled to its protection and to political rights.

civil law. Body of law that deals with the private rights of individuals, as distinguished from criminal law.

civil liberties. Areas of personal freedom with which governments are constrained from interfering.

civil rights. Protections and privileges given to all U.S. citizens by the Constitution and Bill of rights.

civil rights laws. Laws passed by Congress or state legislatures designed to protect the rights of individuals to fair treatment by private persons, groups, organizations, businesses, and government.

civil rights movements. Continuing efforts to gain the enforcement of the rights guaranteed to all citizens by the Constitution.

Civil War Amendments. Thirteenth, Fourteenth, and Fifteenth Amendments, passed following the Civil War. They freed the slaves, granted them citizenship, and guaranteed them the rights of citizens.

class system. System in which members of social classes are prevented from moving into other classes.

clear and present danger. Standard used to justify limitations on speech that will lead directly to harm to others.

colonial charters. Documents granting authority to the original colonies by the British.

common law. Body of unwritten law developed in England from judicial decisions based on custom and earlier judicial decisions. It constitutes the basis of the English legal system and became part of American law.

common or public good. Benefit or interest of a politically organized society as a whole.

compact. See covenant.

concurrent powers. Powers that may be exercised by both the federal government and the state governments—for example, levying taxes, borrowing money, and spending for the general welfare.

consent of the governed. Agreement by the people to set up and live under a government. According to the natural rights philosophy, all legitimate government must rest on the consent of the governed.

constitutionalism. Idea that the powers of government should be distributed according to a written or unwritten constitution and that those powers should be effectively restrained by the constitution's provisions.

covenant. Binding agreement made by two or more persons or parties; compact.

criminal law. Branch of law that deals with disputes or actions involving criminal penalties (as opposed to civil law), it regulates the conduct of individuals, defines crimes, and provides punishment for criminal acts.

delegated powers. Powers granted to the national government under the Constitution, as enumerated in Articles I, II, and III.

democracy. Form of government in which political control is exercised by all the people, either directly or through their elected representatives.

divine right. Theory of government that holds that a monarch receives the right to rule directly from God and not from the people.

domestic tranquility. Internal peacefulness; lack of disturbance within a country.

due process of law. Right of every citizen to be protected against arbitrary action by government.

English Bill of Rights. An act passed by Parliament in 1689 which limited the power of the monarch. This document established Parliament as the most powerful branch of the English government.

enumerated powers. Powers that are specifically granted to Congress by Article I, Section 8 of the Constitution.

equal protection clause. Fourteenth Amendment provision that prohibits states from denying equal protection of the laws to all people—that is, discriminating against individuals in an arbitrary manner, such as on the basis of race.

equal protection of the law. Idea that no individual or group may receive special privileges from nor be unjustly discriminated against by the law.

Equal Rights Amendment (ERA). Placed before Congress in 1923, the ERA stated that "Equal rights under the law shall not be denied or abridged by the United States or any State on account of sex." ERA passed Congress in 1972, but the required three-quarters of the states failed to ratify it. Time for its adoption expired in 1982.

equality of opportunity. An equal chance for all persons in such areas as education, employment, and political participation.

established church or established religion. Official, state-sponsored religion.

establishment clause. Clause in the First Amendment that says the government may not set up, or establish, an official religion.

ethnicity. Group of people that can be identified within a larger culture or society on the basis of such factors as religion, ancestry, or language.

European Union (EU). Successor organization to the "European Community," itself successor to the European Economic Community (EEC), also known as the European "Common Market."

excise taxes. Taxes on the manufacture, sale, or consumption of a manufactured article within a country.

exclusionary rule. Judicial doctrine based on the Fourth Amendment's protection against illegal searches and seizures, which provides that evidence obtained illegally may not be used in a trial.

executive power. Power of the president to implement and enforce laws.

federal judiciary. Nine members of the U.S. Supreme Court and approximately five hundred judges appointed by the president and approved by the Senate for the federal courts created by Congress. The judges are divided among ninety-four district courts and twelve courts of appeal (the "constitutional courts") and a number of specialized courts, such as tax and military courts (the "legislative courts").

federal supremacy clause. Article VI of the Constitution providing that the Constitution and all federal laws and treaties shall be the "supreme Law of the Land." Therefore, all federal laws take precedence over state and local laws.

federal system (or federalism). Form of political organization in which governmental power is divided between a central government and territorial subdivisions—in the United States, among the national, state, and local governments.

federalists. Advocates of a strong national government and supporters of adoption of the U.S. Constitution.

feudalism. Political and economic system in which a king or queen shared power with the nobility who required services from the common people in return for allowing them to use the noble's land.

foreign policy. Policies of the federal government directed to matters beyond U.S. borders, especially relations with other countries. Much domestic policy has foreign policy implications.

Founders. People who played important roles in the development of the national government of the United States.

Framers. Delegates to the Philadelphia Convention held in 1787 and those who wrote and ratified the Bill of Rights.

franchise. Right to vote.

free exercise clause. Clause in the First Amendment that says the government shall make no law prohibiting the free practice of religious beliefs.

freedom of assembly. Freedom of people to gather together in public.

freedom of conscience. Freedom of belief. Many consider freedom of conscience an absolute right, one that has no limitations.

freedom of expression. Refers to the freedoms of speech, press, assembly, and petition that are protected by the First Amendment.

freedom of petition. Freedom to present requests to the government without reprisal.

freedom of the press. Freedom to print or publish without government interference.

freedom of religion. Freedom to worship as one pleases.

freedom of speech. Freedom to express oneself, either verbally or non-verbally, that is, symbolically.

fundamental rights. Rights considered to be essential.

general welfare. Good of society as a whole; common or public good.

general welfare clause. Clause in Article I, Section 8 of the Constitution that gives Congress power to provide for "the general welfare of the United States."

government. Institutions and procedures through which a territory and its people are ruled.

habeas corpus. Court order demanding that the individual in custody be brought into court and shown the cause for detention. *Habeas corpus* is guaranteed by the Constitution and can be suspended only in cases of rebellion or invasion.

"hate" speech. Speech that is intentionally deeply offensive to a racial, ethnic, religious, or other group, seeking to condemn or dehumanize members of such a group.

higher law. In describing a legal system, refers to the superiority of one set of laws over another. For example, the Constitution is a higher law than any federal or state law. In natural rights philosophy, it means that natural law and divine law are superior to laws made by human beings.

House of Commons. One of two houses of the English Parliament; represents the common people.

House of Lords. One of two houses of the English Parliament, represents the nobility.

ideology. Combined doctrines, assertions, and intentions of a social or political group that justify its behavior.

impeachment. Power of Congress to remove the president, vice president, federal judges, and other federal officers from office.

incorporation. Process by which the Supreme Court interpreted the Fourteenth Amendment to extend the Bill of Rights to include protections against actions of the state governments.

individual rights. Rights possessed by individuals as opposed to those rights claimed by groups.

institution (political). Organizations such as Congress, the presidency, and the court system that play a significant role in the making, carrying out, and enforcing laws and managing conflicts about them.

interest group. Organized body of individuals who share some goals and try to influence public policy to meet those goals.

international law. Customs, treaties, agreements, and rules that govern relations among nations.

judicial power. Power to manage conflicts about the interpretation and application of the law.

judicial review. Doctrine that permits the federal courts to declare unconstitutional, and thus null and void, acts of the Congress, the executive, and the states. The precedent for judicial review was established in the 1803 case of *Marbury v. Madison.*

junta. Group of persons controlling a government, especially after a revolutionary seizure of power.

justice. Fair distribution of benefits and burdens, fair correction of wrongs and injuries, or use of fair procedures in gathering information and making decisions

law of nature (or natural law). As used by natural rights philosophers—a moral rule discovered by the use of reason, which everyone should obey at all times and places.

legislative power. Power to make laws.

legitimacy. Acceptance as right and proper.

loyal opposition. Idea that opposition to a government is legitimate; organized opponents to the government of the day.

Magna Carta. Document signed by King John of England in 1215 A.D. that guaranteed certain basic rights. Considered the beginning of constitutional government in England.

majority rule. Rule by more than half of those participating in a decision

Marbury v. Madison (1803). Case in which the Supreme Court held that it had the power of judicial review over acts of Congress.

Marshall Plan. U.S. foreign policy, named after Secretary of State, George C. Marshall, which gave substantial aid to Western European countries after World War II (1948-52) to rehabilitate their economies, ensuring the survival of democratic institutions.

Mayflower Compact. Document drawn up by the Pilgrims in 1620 while on *The Mayflower* before landing at Plymouth Rock. The Compact provided a legal basis for self-government.

minority rights. Rights of any group less than a majority.

monarchy. Government in which political power is exercised by a single ruler under the claim of divine or hereditary right.

national security. Condition of a nation's safety from threats, especially threats from external sources

natural rights. Belief that individuals are naturally endowed with basic human rights; those rights that are so much a part of human nature that they cannot be taken away or given up, as opposed to rights conferred by law. The Declaration of Independence states that these natural rights include the rights to "Life, Liberty and the pursuit of Happiness."

Nineteenth Amendment. Amendment to the Constitution, ratified in 1920, guaranteeing women the right to vote.

Ninth Amendment. This amendment states, in effect, that the Bill of Rights is only a partial listing of the people's rights.

nobility. Group of persons having legally recognized titles, usually of a hereditary nature, who compose the aristocracy in a society. In Great Britain, the nobility is represented in the House of Lords.

OAS. Organization of American States, an international governmental organization formed by the states of North and South America for the protection of mutual security and interests.

political culture. Fundamental beliefs and assumptions of a people about how government and politics should operate.

political efficacy. Belief that one can be effective and have an impact on public affairs.

political ideology. Organized, coherent set of attitudes about government and public policy.

political party. Any group, however loosely organized, that seeks to elect government officials under a given label.

political philosophy. Study of ideas about government and politics.

political rights. Rights to participate in the political process.

preamble. Introduction to a formal document that explains its purpose.

principle. Basic rule that guides or influences thought or action.

private (or personal) domain. Areas of an individual's life that are not subject to governmental control.

private property. Property belonging to a particular person or persons as opposed to the public or the government.

public good. See common good.

public service. Service to local, state, or national communities through appointed or elected office.

Puritan ethic. Belief in the primacy of religious duty, work, conscience, and self-restraint in the life of the individual. Traditionally associated with economic individualism.

representative democracy. Form of government in which power is held by the people and exercised indirectly through elected representatives who make decisions.

republican government. System of government in which power is held by the voters and is exercised by elected representatives responsible for promoting the common welfare.

revolution. Complete or drastic change of government and the rules by which government is conducted.

Roman Republic. Society whose origins were in Rome, dating from 509 B.C. to 27 B.C. Rome served as the model for the theory of classical republicanism.

royalty. Kings, queens, and members of their families. Royalty can also refer to that part of the government that represents the monarch.

rule of law. Principle that every member of a society, even a ruler, must follow the law.

Center for Civic Education

"rule of men." Ability of government officials and others to govern by their personal whim or desire. Opposed to the "rule of law."

separation of church and state. Concept that religion and government should be separate; basis for the establishment clause of the First Amendment.

separation of powers. Division of governmental power among several institutions that must cooperate in decision making.

social contract (compact). Agreement among all the people in a society to give up part of their freedom to a government in return for protection of their natural rights. A theory developed by Locke to explain the origin of legitimate government.

social equality. Absence of inherited or assigned titles of nobility or of a hierarchical caste or class social system.

sovereignty. Ultimate, supreme power in a state; in the United States, sovereignty rests with the people.

suffrage. Right to vote.

supremacy clause. Article VI, Section 2, of the Constitution, which states that the Constitution, laws passed by Congress, and treaties of the United States "shall be the supreme law of the land," binding on the states.

time, place, and manner restrictions. Government regulations which place restrictions on free speech. These regulations, specifying when, where, and in what way speech is allowed, are applied when unrestricted free speech will conflict with the rights of others.

treaty. Formal agreement between sovereign nations to create or restrict rights and responsibilities. In the U.S. all treaties must be approved by a two-thirds vote in the Senate.

"unalienable" (inalienable) rights. Fundamental rights of the people that may not be taken away. A phrase used in the Virginia Declaration of Rights and the Declaration of Independence.

unenumerated rights. Rights which are not specifically listed in the Constitution or Bill of Rights, but which have been recognized and protected by the courts.

unitary government. A government system in which all governmental authority is vested in a central government from which regional and local governments derive their powers. Examples are Great Britain and France, as well as the American states within their spheres of authority.

United Nations. International organization comprising most of the nations of the world, formed in 1945 to promote peace, security, and economic development.

Universal Declaration of Human Rights. International declaration of rights adopted by the United Nations in 1948.

veto. Constitutional power of the president to refuse to sign a bill passed by Congress, thereby preventing it from becoming a law. The president's veto may be overridden by a two-thirds vote of both the Senate and House of Representatives.

World Court. Court in The Hague, the Netherlands, set up by the United Nations Treaty to which nations may voluntarily submit disputes.

Committees and Review Panels

The Center is also grateful for the many helpful comments and suggestions that have been received from the following persons who have reviewed the manuscript in its various developmental stages. The final product, however, is the responsibility of the Center and does not necessarily reflect the views of those who have contributed their thoughts and ideas.

STANDARDS STEERING COMMITTEE

William G. Baker, Esq., Former Chairperson, Governors Task Force on Citizenship Education State of Indiana

Jean B. Elshtain, Professor Political Science Department Vanderbilt University

William F. Harris, Professor Department of Political Science University of Pennsylvania

A.E. Dick Howard, Professor School of Law, University of Virginia

Stephen Macedo, Michael O. Sawyer Professor of Constitutional Law and Politics Syracuse University

Sheilah Mann, Director of Education Affairs, American Political Science Association

Milton D. Morris, Vice President for Office of Research Joint Center for Political and Economic Studies

Walter F. Murphy McCormick Professor of Jurisprudence, Princeton University

James Nathan, Khalid bin Sultan Eminent Scholar, Auburn University at Montgomery

Ruth Wattenberg, Associate Director, Educational Issues Department, American Federation of Teachers

Linda Williams, Professor Department of Government and Politics, University of Maryland

Ex Officio:

Anne Fickling, Program Officer Office of Educational Research and Improvement, U.S. Department of Education

NATIONAL ADVISORY COMMITTEE

Gordon M. Ambach, Executive Director, Council of Chief State School Officers

Charlotte Anderson, President Education for Global Involvement

William G. Baker, Esq. Chairperson, Governors Task Force on Citizenship Education State of Indiana

Alvin Bell, Teacher Findlay High School, Ohio

Peter Benda, Associate for Public Policy, The Pew Charitable Trusts

Diane E. Bolander, Director Legislative Service Bureau

R. Freeman Butts, William F. Russell Professor Emeritus in the Foundations of Education Teachers College, Columbia University

Robert Chase, Vice President National Education Association

John F. Cooke, President The Disney Channel

Thomas H. Dawson Administrative Assistant, Office of The Honorable Neal Smith U.S. House of Representatives

Jean B. Elshtain, Professor Political Science Department Vanderbilt University

Patton L. Feichter, Teacher Maine South High School, Illinois

Paul Gagnon, Senior Associate National Education Commission on Time and Learning

William F. Harris, Professor Department of Political Science University of Pennsylvania

Andrew J. Hartman, Minority Staff Director, Committee on Education and Labor, U.S. House of Representatives

A. E. Dick Howard, Professor School of Law, University of Virginia

Karl Kurtz, Director of State Services, National Conference of State Legislatures

Martharose Laffey, Executive Director, National Council for Social Studies

Sheilah Mann, Director of Education Affairs, American Political Science Association

Milton D. Morris, Vice President for Office of Research Joint Center for Political and Economic Studies

Walter F. Murphy, McCormick Professor of Jurisprudence Princeton University

James Nathan, Khalid bin Sultan Eminent Scholar, Auburn University at Montgomery

Henry A. Neil, Jr., Staff Assistant Retired, Subcommittee on Labor, Health and Human Services and Education, U.S. House of Representatives

John J. Patrick, Director, Social Studies Development Center Indiana University

Richard Remy, Associate Director The Mershon Center Ohio State University

Roger Rogalin, Vice President School Division, Association of American Publishers, Inc.

Raymond W. Smock, Historian U.S. House of Representatives

John W. Turcotte, Executive Director, Joint PEER Committee National Conference of State Legislatures

Reed Ueda, Professor, Department of History, Tufts University

Ruth Wattenberg, Associate Director, Educational Issues Department, American Federation of Teachers

Ex Officio:
Jan Anderson, Director, Fund for the Improvement and Reform of Schools and Teaching Board U.S. Department of Education

Anne Fickling, Program Officer Office of Educational Research and Improvement, U.S. Department of Education

NATIONAL REVIEW COMMITTEE

John Allen, Director of Programs National 4-H Council

Gordon M. Ambach, Executive Director, Council of Chief State School Officers

Joan Chikos Auchter, Director of Test Development, The General Educational Development Testing Service of the American Council on Education

Tyrone Ayers, Director, Planning Division, U.S. Internal Revenue Services

Richard D. Bagin, Executive Director, National School Public Relations Association

Christine Becker, National League of Cities

John G. Blanche III, Executive Staff Director, Federal Bar Association

Frederick Brigham, Jr., Special Assistant to the President National Catholic Education Association

David Browne, Planning Officer Internal Revenue Service Planning Division

The Honorable John H. Buchanan Jr., Senior Vice President People for the American Way

Gene Carter, Executive Director Association for Supervision and Curriculum Development

Michael Casserly, Executive Director, Council of the Great City Schools

JoAnn Chase, Executive Director National Congress of American Indians

Gloria Chernay, Executive Director, Association of Teacher Educators

Todd Clark, Executive Director Constitutional Rights Foundation

Tom Cochran, Executive Director U.S. Conference of Mayors

Maudine Cooper, President and Chief Executive Officer Washington Urban League

Carolyn Crider, Executive Director, National Independent Private School Association

Fred Czarra, Consultant, Council of Chief State School Officers

Gail Donovan, Commission on National and Community Service

Timothy Dyer, Executive Director National Association of Secondary School Principals

Edward Ferguson, Deputy Executive Director, National Association of Counties

Paul Gagnon, Senior Associate National Education Commission on Time and Learning

Matt Gandal, American Federation of Teachers

Christopher T. Gates Vice President, National Civic League

Keith Geiger, President, National Education Association

James R. Giese, Executive Director, Social Science Education Consortium, Inc

Jack C. Hanna, Project Director, Phi Alpha Delta Public Service Center

Rachel Hicks, Director of Public Relations and Staff Development Washington D.C. Teachers Union

Gracia M. Hillman, Executive Director, The League of Women Voters of the United States

Joyce D. Hoover, Social Studies Test Specialist, The General Educational Development Testing Service of the American Council on Education

Paul Houston, Executive Director, American Association of School Administrators

David Imig, Executive Director American Association of Colleges for Teacher Education

Rebecca Isaacs, Legislative Counsel, People for the American Way

Clifford B. Janey, Chief Academic Officer, Boston School Department

Stephen A. Janger, President Close Up Foundation

Enid Jones, Clearinghouse Manager, Quality Education for Minorities Network

Lois Jordan, Chairperson, Social Studies, Pearl Cohen Comprehensive High School

James A. Kelly, President
National Board for Professional
Standards

Martharose Laffey, Executive
Director, National Council for
Social Studies

Michael Lin, National Vice
President for Education and
Culture Organization of Chinese
Americans

Gary Marx, Associate Executive
Director, American Association of
School Administrators

Joyce G. McCray, Executive
Director, Council for American
Private Education

Mabel McKinney-Browning
Director, Division for Public
Eucation, American Bar
Association

Milton Mitler, Vice President and
Public Information Liaison, U.S.
Chamber of Commerce

Mario Moreno, Regional Counsel
Mexican American Legal Defense
Fund

Karen Narasaki, Representative
Japanese American Citizens
League

Betty Neesen, Manager of
Program Planning, National 4-H
Council

Jason Newman, Director
National Institute for Citizen
Education in Law

John Parr, President, National
Civic League

Robert Pickus, President, World
Without War Council

Helen W. Richardson, Executive
Director for Secondary
Curriculum, Fulton County School
System

Dr. Santee Ruffin, Executive
Director, National Alliance of
Black School Educators

Samuel G. Sava, Executive
Director, National Association of
Elementary School Principals

Jeffrey Schiff, Executive Director
National Association of Town and
Townships

Gilbert Sewall, Executive
Director, American Textbook
Council

Albert Shanker, President
American Federation of Teachers

Thomas A. Shannon, Executive
Director, National School Boards
Association

Andrew Smith, President
American Forum

Mary Soley, Representative
United States Institute of Peace

Betty L. Sullivan
Director, Education Programs
Newspaper Association of America

Sue Swain, Executive Director
National Middle School
Association

Susan Traiman, Director
Education Initiative, The
Business Roundtable

Carl Tubbesing, Director
Legislatures, National Conference
of State Legislatures

Kathryn Whitfill, President,
National PTA

NATIONAL SCHOLARS
REVIEW PANEL

Herbert Atherton, Consultant

James M. Banner, Jr., Director of
Academic Programs, James
Madison Memorial Fellowship
Foundation

Herman Belz, Professor
Department of History
University of Maryland

Harry Boyte, Senior Fellow
Hubert Humphrey Institute of
Public Affairs, University of
Minnesota

Walter Enloe, Assistant Director
Institute for International
Studies, University of Minnesota

Russell Farnen, Professor
Department of Political Science
University of Connecticut

Chester E. Finn, Jr., Founding
Partner and Director of
Government Relations, The
Edison Project

John D. Fonte, Educational
Consultant

Paul Gagnon, Senior Associate
National Education Commission
on Time and Learning

Norman N. Gill, Scholar,
Marquette University

Douglas Imig, Visiting Scholar
PNS Center for International
Affairs, Harvard University

John Kincaid, Executive Director
Advisory Commission on
Intergovernmental Relations

Harvey C. Mansfield, Professor
Department of Government
Harvard University

James G. Shriner, Professor
Department of Education
Clemson University

Philippa Strum, Professor
Department of Political Science
Brooklyn College of the City
University of New York

David Vogler, Professor
Department of Political Science
Wheaton College

Linda Williams, Professor
Department of Government and
Politics, University of Maryland

NATIONAL CONFERENCE OF STATE LEGISLATURES CIVIC EDUCATION TASK FORCE

Diane Bolender, **Chair**, Director
Legislative Service Bureau, Iowa

Charlotte Kerr, **Vice Chair**
Chief Legislative Analyst, Joint
Legislative Audit and Review
Commission, Virginia

Terry Anderson, Director
Legislative Research Council
South Dakota

Toni Christman, Administrative
Assistant to the Republican
Caucas Administrator, House of
Representatives, Pennsylvania

Richard Johnson
Deputy Director
Legislative Service Bureau, Iowa

Karl Kurtz, Director of State
Services, National Conference of
State Legislatures, Colorado

Gary Olson, Director
Senate Fiscal Agency, Michigan

Susan Seladones, Director of
Public Affairs, National
Conference of State Legislatures,
Washington, District of Columbia

Richard Strong, Director and
General Counsel, Office of
Legislative Research, Utah

John Turcotte, Executive Director
Joint PEER Committee
Mississippi

INTERNATIONAL REVIEWERS

Attila Agh, Professor, Department
of Political Science, Budapest
University of Economic Sciences
Hungary

Mihály Benedek, Editor
Nemzeti Tankönyvkiadó Rt.
Hungary

Wolfgang Böge, Professor
Department of Education,
Universität der Bundeswehr
Hamburg, Federal Republic of
Germany

Vladislovas Budzinauskas, Senior
Officer, Social Sciences Division,
Ministry of Education and
Science, Lithuania

John Carter, Director
Parliamentary Education Office
Australia

Vincenzo Consiglio, Consigliere
Ministeriale Aggiunto, Ministero
della Pubblica Istruzione, Italy

Karlheinz Dürr, Professor
Deutsches Institut für
Fernstudienforschung der
Universität Tübingen, Federal
Republic of Germany

Glória Garcia, Professor
Department of Law and Politics
Universidade Católica Portuguesa
Portugal

Irmgard Hantsche, Professor
Department of History
Universität Duisburg, Federal
Republic of Germany

Marie Houmerouá, Teacher
Gymnázium Jana Keplera, Czech
Republic

Dietmar Kahsnitz, Professor
Institut für
Polytechnik/Arbeitslehre
J.W. Goethe-Universität
Frankfurt am Main, Federal
Republic of Germany

Jaroslav Kalous, Director
Center for Educational
Development, Charles University
Czech Republic

Jaroslav Marek Klejnocki
Lecturer, University of Warsaw
Poland

Barbara Malak-Minkiewicz,
Consultant, Polish Ministry of
Education, Department of Teacher
Training, The Netherlands

Silvia Matúšová, Professor
Ústredné Metodické Centrum
Slovakia

Ivo Mozny, Chairman
Department of Sociology, Social
Work and Policy, Masaryk
University, Czech Republic

Henryk Palkij, Director, Center
for Civic and Economic Education
Poland

Ylli Pango, Deputy Minister of
Education, Albanian Ministry of
Education, Albania

Horst Pötzsch, Ltd.
Regierungsdirektor Bundeszentrale
für politische Bildung, Federal
Republic of Germany

Douglas Ramsey, Specialist
Social Studies, Calgary Board of
Education, Canada

Bozo Repe, Professor, Department
of Modern History, University of
Maribor, Slovenia

Salvador E. Stadthagen, Director
Programa de Educacion para la
Democracia, Nicaragua

Jacek Strzemieczny, Director
Center for Citizenship Education
Poland

Paul Tarábek, Publisher,
DIDAKTIS, Slovakia

Soledad Teixido, Director, Civic
Education Programs for
Elementary and Secondary Levels
Participa, Chile

Anca Tirca, Consultant Romanian
Independent Society for Human
Rights, Romania

Rolf Th. Tønnessen, Professor
Kristiansand College of Education
Norway

Anita Ushacka, Professor
University of Latvia Law School
Latvia

Hartmut Wasser, Professor
Department of Political Science
Pädagogische Hochschule
Weingarten, Federal Republic of
Germany

Michael G. Watt, Consultant
Tasmania, Australia

Edmund Wnuk-Lipinski, Director
Institute of Political Studies
Polish Academy of Sciences
Poland

Center for Civic Education

Jan Wrobel, Teacher of History and School Board Member, First Communal High School, Poland

COUNCIL OF STATE SOCIAL STUDIES SPECIALISTS (CS4) REVIEW PANEL STEERING COMMITTEE

California:
Diane Brooks, Manager History-Social Science Unit California State Education Department

Florida:
Tom Dunthorn, Social Studies Consultant, Florida Department of Education

Kansas:
Richard D. Leighty, Social Studies Specialist, Kansas State Board of Education

Missouri:
Warren H. Solomon, Curriculum Consultant for Social Studies Missouri State Department of Elementary and Secondary Education

New Hampshire:
Carter B. Hart, Jr., Curriculum Supervisor, New Hampshire Department of Education

New Jersey:
Paul Cohen, Principal, Constable Elementary School

North Carolina:
John D. Ellington, Program Consultant, North Carolina Department of Public Instruction

Ohio:
Kent J. Minor, Social Studies Consultant, Ohio Department of Education

Oklahoma:
Rita Geiger, Coordinator, Social Studies, Oklahoma State Education Department

Texas:
Elvin E. Tyrone Education Specialist Texas Education Agency

NATIONAL EVALUATION PANEL

Joan Herman, Associate Director Center for the Study of Evaluation/Center for Research on Evaluation, Standards, and Student Testing (CSE/CRESST) University of California at Los Angeles

Pete Kneedler, Consultant California Department of Education

Ruth Mitchell, Associate Director Council for Basic Education

Dan Resnick Director of Development New Standards Project

TEACHER REVIEW PANELS

Alabama:
Sue Powell, Hoover
Roger Tyner, Maylene

Alaska:
Donald L. Surgeon, Sitka

Arizona:
Lisa K. Adams, Phoenix

Arkansas:
Larry Cochran, Fort Smith
Liz Fitzhugh, Malvern

California:
Doreen Aghajanian, Canoga Park
Beth Arner, Bakersfield
Marvin Awbrey, Fresno
Ed Burke, Chatsworth
Mary Kathleen Chagnovich
    Rancho Palos Verdes
Arleen Chatman, Los Angeles
Minnie Crews, Los Angeles
Ed Graham, Long Beach
Nancy Henry, Lakewood
Pat Husain, El Segundo
Sue Keavney, Arcadia
Henry Legere, Los Alamitos
Gary Marksbury, Long Beach
Nancy Miller, Oceanside
Ron Morris, Arcadia
David N. Richmond, Bakersfield
Barbara Vallejo-Doten
    Long Beach
Marilyn Washington, Los Angeles

Colorado:
Phyllis Clarke Bye, Boulder
Jackie Johnson, Englewood
Ginny Jones, Boulder

Connecticut:
Sharon Moran, Manchester

Delaware:
Becky Burton, Georgetown
Francis J. O'Malley, Wilmington
Gerald T. Peden, Georgetown

District of Columbia:
Shirley Powe, Washington
Mary Douglas Reed, Washington

Florida:
James J. Elliott, Winter Springs
Judy Nugent, Sebring
David John Stump, Naples

Georgia:
Rebecca Sykes Chambers, Decatur
Betsy King, Clarkesville
Tim Watkins, Lawrenceville
William W. Bradley, Atlanta

Hawaii:
Sue Ann Chun, Wahiawa
Julie Kaohi-Matsumoto, Honolulu
Linda Smith, Laie

Idaho:
Vera Lynn Geer, Twin Falls

Illinois:
James Conrad, Hinsdale
Victoria E. Goben, Wheaton
Stan Mendenhall, Pekin
Jerry Sax, Gridley

Indiana:
Mark Sausser, Indianapolis

Iowa:
Dennis Albertson, Ankeny
Donna McClure, Grimes
Jodie Reagan, Grimes

Kansas:
Jane Bennington, St. John
Judy Daeschner, Topeka
Cheryl Serer, Russell

Kentucky:
Libby Gooch, Madisonville
Mike Haile, Henderson
Sandra D. Hoover, Louisville

Louisiana:
Anna Hinson, Baker
Judy S. Lucius, Baton Rouge
Alice S. Wallace, Baton Rouge

Maine:
David Ezhaya, Windham
Claire Lambert, Westbrook
Dan Madden, Bath

Maryland:
Rosemary V. Miller, Annapolis
Linda A. Satterthwaite, Fort
Washington

Massachusetts:
Roger L. Desrosiers, Millbury

Michigan:
Deborah Snow, Grand Rapids

Mississippi:
Mary Alexander, Poplarville
Cheri Ladner, Long Beach
Pamela Manners, Biloxi

Missouri:
Judy Burnette, St. Louis
Ed Richardson, Kansas City
Charles Spradling, Joplin

Nebraska:
Sue McNeil, Taylor

Nevada:
Denton Gehr, Sparks

New Hampshire:
Bill Hixon, Bethlehem
Laura McCrillis-Kessler, Hillsboro
Joel Mitchell, Brookline

New Jersey:
Ruth Coakley, Succasunna
Doug Martin, Trenton
Elizabeth Snyder, Succasunna

New Mexico:
Keith Neel, Tijeras

New York:
Leo Casey, Brooklyn
Henry Mueller, Niskayuna
Judith S. Wooster, Delmar

North Carolina:
Katherine Dunn, Greensboro
Kara Lee Little, Lexington
Christine Youmans, Pleasant
Garden

North Dakota:
Chris Deuthit, Grand Forks
Dan Vainonen, Jamestown
Janice Wahl, Fargo

Ohio:
Tina Beck, Columbus
Clotilda Krivda, Columbus
Teresa Lonsbury, Centerville

Oklahoma:
Ronny Babione, Altus
Carolyn White, Idabel
Emily Wood, Tulsa

Oregon:
Bob Bass, Roseburg
Kay Fry, Eugene
Theresa Murray, Portland

Pennsylvania:
Debra Drossner, Maple Glen
Jim Gavahan, Abington
Paul R. Pryor, Upper St. Clair

Rhode Island:
Andy Robinson, Point Judith
Michael Trofi, West Warwick
Denise Zavota, East Providence

South Carolina:
Marsha Burch, Florence

South Dakota:
Kathryn Griffin, Aberdeen
Roland Storly, Aberdeen

Tennessee:
Mary Catherine Bradshaw
 Nashville
Holly West Brewer, Joelton
Mari Essery, Nashville

Texas:
Ali Dailey, Austin
Patricia Dobbs, Austin
Jeanne M. Slaydon, Houston

Utah:
Glenn V. Bird, Springville
Patsy T. Bueno, Price
Krista Tharnack, Provo

Virginia:
Barbara Dalle Mura, Richmond
Conde Hopkins, Ashland
Barbara Lester, Norfolk

Washington:
Steve Antles, Auburn
Janet Slezak, Des Moines
Kay Stern, Ridgefield

West Virginia:
Linda Crim, Martinsburg
Barbara Iaquinta, Nutter Fort
Laura Rush, Princeton
Jennie Shaffer, Keyser
Linda Smith, Barboursville

Wisconsin:
Kurt Bergland, Wauwatosa
Ann Christianson, Wausau
Rob Rauh, Milwaukee

Wyoming:
Dick J. Kean, Jr., Cheyenne

STATE REVIEW COMMITTEES

Alabama:
Chairperson:
Janice Loomis, Program
Consultant, Alabama Center for
Law & Civic Education
Committee:
Betty Burtram, Corner High
School
Tavis Hardin, North Birmingham
Elementary
Martha McInnish, Madison
County Schools
Peggy Nikolakis
Mobile County Public Schools
Robert Summerville, State of
Alabama, Department of
Education

Alaska:
Chairperson:
Marjorie Menzi, Curriculum
Specialist, Social Studies, Alaska
Department of Education
Committee:
Mary Bristol, Anchorage Schools
Lynndeen Knapp, Houston Jr./Sr.
High School
Terry Martin, Alaska State
Legislature
Doug Phillips, Anchorage School
District
Linda Raemaeker, Skyview High
School
Cathy Walter, Colony Middle School

Arizona:
Chairperson:
Lynda Rando, Director, Arizona
Center for Law-Related Education

Committee:
Ray Chavez, Sunnyside School District
Charlotte Madden, Flagstaff High School
Bob White, Consultant
Mary Williams, Laveen High School

Arkansas:
Chairperson:
Barbara Stafford, Executive Director, Learning Law in Arkansas
Committee:
Leon Adams, Little Rock School District
Robin May, Sherwood Elementary School
Rebecca Revis, Sylvan Hills Junior High School
Patricia Roach, Arkansas Tech University
David Sink, University of Arkansas Little Rock

California:
Chairperson:
Diane Brooks, Manager History-Social Science Unit California State Education Department
Committee:
Ira Clark, California Department of Education
Chris Flannery, Azusa Pacific University
John Hyland, Los Angeles Unified School District
Jean McDaniel, Elk Grove Unified School District
John Robertson, Glendale Unified School District
David Vigilante, San Diego Unified School District

Colorado:
Chairperson:
Barbara Miller, Program Consultant
Committee:
Barbara Conroy, Adams 14 School District
Loyal Darr, Denver Public Schools

Marianne Kenney, Curriculum and Instruction Unit, Colorado Department of Education
Brian D. Loney, Law-Related Education Project, Jefferson County Schools
Lauri McNown, Kittridge Honors Program, University of Colorado
Christine Northrop, Colorado Bar Association
Rebecca Virtue, Colorado Judicial Department, Office of the State Court Administrator

Connecticut:
Chairperson:
Daniel Gregg, Social Studies Consultant, Department of Education
Committee:
Margaret Andrews, Kennelly School
Edward Sembor, Jr., University of Connecticut
Benjamin Skaught, Conard High School
Marina Taverne, Norwalk Public Schools
Thomas P. Weinland, University of Connecticut

Delaware:
Chairperson:
Lewis E. Huffman, State Social Studies Supervisor, Department of Public Instruction
Committee:
Becky Burton, Georgetown Elementary School
Margaret M. Loveland, Department of Public Instruction
Lewis Miller, Caesar Rodney School District
Thomas Neubauer Middletown High School
Steven Newton Delaware State University

Florida:
Chairperson:
Tom Dunthorn
Social Studies Consultant Florida Department of Education
Committee:
Randall G. Felton Leon County Schools

Sheila F. Keller Florida Department of Education
Annette Boyd Pitts Florida LRE Association
Gemma Santos Coral Gables Senior High School
Jeanne Shabazz John Stockton Elementary School
Theron L. Trimble Collier County Public Schools

Georgia:
Chairperson:
Michelle Collins, Consultant Northwest Georgia Regional Education Service Agency
Committee:
Rebecca Sykes Chambers Clarkston High School
Wayne Huntley Floyd County Schools
Jerry Raymond Gwinnett County Schools
Helen S. Ridley Department of Political Science Kennesaw State College

Hawaii:
Chairperson:
Sharon Kaohi, Coordinator Hawaii Department of Education
Committee:
Deborah Hall, Iolani School
Lyle Hendricks Farrington High School
Jane Kinoshita Department of Education
Kim Noveloso Ewa Beach Elementary School
Mitch Yamasaki Chaminade University
Sandy Young, Kamehameha Schools, Bishop Estate

Idaho:
Chairperson:
George Gates, Professor of Education, Idaho State University, College of Education
Committee:
David Adler Idaho State University
David J. Case Blackfoot School District #55
Vera Lynn Geer Sawtooth Elementary School

Sally J. Pena
Idaho State University

Dan Prinzing
Les Bois Junior High School

Steve Tyree
Boise School District #1

Illinois:
Chairperson:
Fred Drake, Program Consultant

Committee:
Robert C. Bradley
Illinois State University

John Craig
Illinois State Board of Education

Patton Feichter
Maine South High School

Mindy McMahon
Madison Elementary

Stanley Mendenhall, Edison Jr.
High School and Dirksen Center

Indiana:
Chairperson:
Robert Leming, Director, Social
Studies Development Center
Indiana University

Committee:
Sandra Baker, Elliott School

Rick Borries, Evansville-
Vanderburgh School District

Denee Corbin, School of
Education, Purdue University

Mary Fortney
Indiana Department of Education

The Honorable Paul D. Mathias
Allen County Courthouse

Victor Smith
Riverside Elementary School

Iowa:
Chairperson:
Cordell Svengalis
Social Science Consultant
Department of Education

Committee:
Carol Brown
Des Moines Public Schools

Tim Buzzell
Center for Law and Civic Education

Helen Finken, City High School

Louise Thurn, Keystone AEA 1

John Wheeler
Center for Law and Civic Education

Kansas:
Chairperson:
Richard D. Leighty
Social Studies Specialist
Kansas State Board of Education

Committee:
Judy Cromwell
Topeka Education Center

Cheryl Deck, Oskaloosa High School

Marilyn Geiger
Washburn University

Sharon Hamil
Shawnee Mission USD 512

Debbie McKenna
Gateway Project, Wichita USD 259

Kentucky:
Chairperson:
James Graves
Program Consultant

Committee:
Carol Banks
Franklin County Schools

Nijel Clayton, Kentucky
Department of Education

Tami Dowler
Kentucky Education Association

Nancy Gilligan
Fayette County Public Schools

Derrick W. Graham
Frankfort High School

Diane Hampton
Clay County School System

Joe Lovell, Elkhorn Middle School

Louisiana:
Chairperson:
William J. Miller
Program Manager, Social Studies
State Department of Education

Committee:
John Alexander
Jefferson Parish School Board

Mike Bierman
T.H. Harris Middle School

Christine Jones, Louisiana
Department of Education

James Llorens
Southern University

Patricia Williams, East Baton
Rouge Parish School System
Lee High School

Maine:
Chairperson:
Pamela L. Beal
Program Consultant

Committee:
Anthony Corrado, Department of
Government, Colby College

Kathleen L. Lee
Old Orchard Beach School
Department

Miriam L. Remar, Howard C.
Reiche Community School

Vernon A. Saunders
Falmouth Middle School

Maryland:
Chairperson:
James Adomanis
Program Consultant

Committee:
Linda Adamson, Mayo Elementary

Stephen Barry, Anne Arundel
County Public Schools

Lester Brooks, Anne Arundel
County Community College

Vincent F. Catania
Glenwood Middle School

Phyllis Cherry
Corkran Middle School

Barbara Connolly
Severn River Junior High School

Courtney Finch
Arundel High School

Steve Frantzich
United States Naval Academy

Stephanie Fries
Arundel High School

Robert Jervis, Anne Arundel
County Public Schools

Peg Killam-Smith
St. Mary's Catholic High School

Patricia Lawlor, Parent

Patricia Orndorff, Anne Arundel
County Public Schools

John Richardson
North County High School

Whitman Ridgway, University of
Maryland, College Park

Massachusetts:
Chairperson:
Marjorie A. Montgomery
Program Consultant

Committee:
Rosalie Carter-Dixon
Boston Public Schools

Brian Mooney
Educational Consultant

Larry Scherpa
Birchland Park School

Michigan:

Chairperson:
Linda Start, Executive Director
Michigan Center for Civic
Education Through Law

Committee:
Carol Bacak-Egbo
Waterford School District
Donelson Elementary

Paul Dain, Bloomfield Hills Public
Schools, Andover High School

David Harris, Oakland Schools

Cleotha Jordan
Detroit Public Schools

Michael Yocum, Michigan Council
for Social Studies

Minnesota:

Chairperson:
Roger K. Wangen, International
and Social Studies Education
Specialist, Minnesota Department
of Education

Committee:
Jennifer Bloom, Center for
Community Legal Education,
Hamline Law School

Robert Crumpton, Minnesota
Department of Education

Bob Gabrich
White Bear Lake High School

Cindy Rogers
Minneapolis Public Schools

Mississippi:

Chairperson:
Lynette McBrayer, Director
Mississippi Law-Related
Education Center

Committee:
Andy Armstrong
Newton High School

F.V. Carmichael
Clarkdale Attendance Center

Amy Carpenter, Mississippi Bar

Johnny Gilbert
Bailey Magnet School

Carolyn Lucas
West Bolivar High School

Jack Perry, Gulfport High School

Joann Prewitt, Mississippi
Department of Education

Missouri:

Chairperson:
Warren H. Solomon, Curriculum
Consultant, Social Studies,
Missouri Department of
Elementary and Secondary
Education

Committee:
Brenda Caine, Eldon R-I Schools

Bill Mendelsohn
Clayton School District

Madeleine Schmitt
St. Louis Public Schools

Kathleen Vest
Independence Public Schools

Montana:

Chairperson:
Linda Vrooman-Peterson
Social Studies Specialist, Office of
Public Instruction

Committee:
Larry Fink, Hysham Elementary

Bob Hislop, Polson High School

Marlene LaCounte, Montana
State University-Billings

James J. Lopach
University of Montana

Kathleen Mollahan
Office of Public Instruction

Nebraska:

Chairperson:
Tom Keefe, Director
Nebraska State Bar Association

Committee:
David DeCent
Wilcox Public Schools

James Dick
University of Nebraska at Omaha

Anne Hubbell
Culler Middle School

John LeFeber, Nebraska
Department of Education

Sue McNeil
Loup County Public Schools

Nevada:

Chairperson:
Phyllis Darling, Executive
Director, Nevada Center for
Law-Related Education

Committee:
James W. Lamare
University of Nevada, Las Vegas

Beth Sloan, Western High School

Ann Turner, Greenspun Jr. High

Tony Vicari, Oran Gragson

New Hampshire:

Chairperson:
Carter Hart, Jr., Curriculum
Supervisor, New Hampshire
Department of Education

Committee:
LeRoy C. Ehmling
Hillsboro Deering High School

Sally Jean Jensen
Holderness Central School

David L. Larson
University of New Hampshire

Donald Marquis
Nashua School District

Mark Vallone
Bedford School System

Richard M. Verrill
Milford High School

New Jersey:

Chairperson:
Paul Cohen, South Brunswick
Board of Education

Committee:
Theresa Buela
Quibbletown Middle School

Fred Cotterell
Paramus School District

Kiran T. Handa
Governor's Office of Volunteerism

Joe Kovacs, Benjamin Franklin
Elementary School

Alan Markowitz
Roxbury Twp. Public Schools

Gerald Pomper, Rutgers
University/Eagleton Institute

Ryan Ransom, Edison High School

Mary Ann Savino, Central School

Elaine Spalluto, Trenton

Evelyn Taraszkiewicz
Bayonne Board of Education

Bill Wraga
Bernards Twp. Public Schools

New Mexico:
Chairperson:
Dora Marroquin
Program Consultant

Committee:
Pat Concannon, New Mexico State
Department of Education

Jean Craven
Albuquerque Public Schools

Tom Martin
Gadsden Jr. High School

Lynette K. Oshima
University of New Mexico

Betty L. Waugh, Albuquerque

Norma Zanotelli, Las Cruces

New York:
Chairperson:
Stephen L. Schechter, Director
The Council for Citizenship
Education, Professor, Department
of Political Science, Russell Sage
College, Troy

Committee:
Richard B. Bernstein, Adjunct
Associate Professor of Law, New
York Law School

Lloyd Bromberg, Director of Social
Studies, New York City Board of
Education

George Gregory, Curriculum and
Assessment Team, New York
State Education Department

Eric S. Mondschein, Director
Law, Youth and Citizenship
Program, New York State Bar
Association and New York State
Education Department

Stephanie Schechter
Social Studies Teacher
Niskayuna Middle School

North Carolina:
Chairperson:
John Ellington
Program Consultant

Committee:
Donald Bohlen
Guilford County Schools

Robert (Robin) Dorff
North Carolina State University

Mary Vann Eslinger
North Carolina Department of
Public Instruction Retired

Cynthia Henry
New Hanover County Schools

Kathy Revels, Vandorra Springs
Elementary School and Aversboro
Road Elementary School

Doug Robertson, North Carolina
Department of Public Instruction

North Dakota:
Chairperson:
Phil Harmeson
University of North Dakota

Committee:
Rolland Larson, North Dakota
Department of Public Instruction

Gary Malm
Grand Forks Public Schools

Mary Jane Nudell
Grand Forks Public Schools

Lloyd B. Omdahl
University of North Dakota

Ohio:
Chairperson:
Kent J. Minor
Social Studies Consultant
Ohio Department of Education

Committee:
Beverly Clark
Cleveland City Schools

David T. Naylor
University of Cincinnati

Debra Hallock Phillips, American
New Media Educational
Foundation

Chuck Schierloh
Lima City Schools

Robert B. Woyach
The Mershon Center

Oklahoma:
Chairperson:
Rita Geiger, Coordinator
Social Studies, Oklahoma State
Education Department

Committee:
Gary W. Banz
Midwest City High School

Pam Branham
Edmond High School

Cheryl Franklin, Enid High School

Danney Goble, Carl Albert
Congressional Research and
Study Center, University of
Oklahoma

Dianne E. Hill
Muskogee Public Schools

Oregon:
Chairperson:
Marilyn Cover, Director
Classroom Law Project

Committee:
James Harrison
Portland Public Schools

Karen Hoppes, Oregon Council for
the Social Studies

Tom McKenna, Grant High School

Theresa Murray, Oregon Council
for the Social Studies

Mike Sanderson
Sunset High School

Pennsylvania:
Chairperson:
James Wetzler
Social Studies Consultant
Department of Education

Committee:
Sharon S. Laverdure
J.M. Hill Elementary School

Raymond B. McClain
Pittsburgh Public Schools

Lawrence K. Pettit, Indiana
University of Pennsylvania

Deborah Sagan
Marshall Elementary School
North Allegheny School District

Rhode Island:
Chairperson:
John R. Waycott
Program Consultant

Committee:
Constance A. Barber
East Providence High School

Henry F. Cote
Pawtucket School Department

Diana Crowley, Rhode Island
Department of Education

Rosamond Ethier
Salve Regina University

Kathleen Mospaw
Burrillville Jr. High School

William J. Piacentini
Park View Jr. High School

South Carolina:
Chairperson:
Cindy Coker, Director
Law-Related Education
South Carolina Bar

Committee:
Marsha Burch
Florence School District 1

Sandra Funderburk
Greenville Middle School

Paul Horne
Richland School District 1

Roy M. Stehle
Beaufort County School District

Margaret B. Walden, SERC

South Dakota:
Chairperson:
Lennis Larson
Program Consultant

Committee:
Patrick D. Gainey
Spearfish High School

Todd Hansen
Northern State University

Arthur Marmorstein
Northern State University
Department of History

Dean Myers
Black Hills State University

Tennessee:
Chairperson:
Bruce Opie, Education Program
Administrator, Department of
Education

Committee:
Beth Goforth, Jackson
Central-Merry High School

Haskell Greer, Warren County
Senior High School

Dorothy Skeel, Peabody College of
Vanderbilt University

Thomas C. Vandervort, Middle
Tennessee State University

Malcolm J. Walker
Chattanooga Public Schools

Jamessena Washington
Austin East High School

Texas:
Chairperson:
Elvin E. Tyrone
Education Specialist
Texas Education Agency

Committee:
Elizabeth Battle
Texas Council for Social Studies

Margaret Hamilton
Trinity High School

Sy Karlin, Texas Social Studies
Supervisors Association

Utah:
Chairperson:
Rulon Garfield, Professor of
Educational Leadership

Committee:
Garn Coombs
Brigham Young University

David Crow
Canyon View Junior High

Luan Ferrin
Weber State University

Daniel Hansen
Wilson Elementary School

Diane Hemond, Orem High School

Bonnie Morgan, Utah State Board
of Education

Carol Sullivan, Kanab High School

Carl Yeager
Utah Valley State College

Virginia:
Chairperson:
Helen Coalter
Program Consultant

Committee:
Jack Austin, Virginia
Commonwealth University,
Department of Legislative Services

Lee Chase
Chesterfield County Public Schools

Mark Crockett, Virginia
Department of Education

Marianne Merriman
Huguenot High School

Pam Tuskey
Meadowbrook High School

Washington:
Chairperson:
Kathy Hand
Educational Consultant

Committee:
Sue K. Barnum
Tacoma School District

Elsie H. Cadena
Rogers High School

Peter J. Hovenier
Western Washington University

Donna Janovitch
Washington Middle School

Jim McBride, Wilson Elementary

Jo Rosner, Esq.
Washington State Bar

Larry Strickland, OSPI Office of
Superintendent of Public
Instruction

Roger Westman
Tacoma School District

West Virginia:
Chairperson:
Barbara Jones, Social Studies
Coordinator West Virginia
Department of Education

Committee:
Frances Gunter
Milton High School

Evelyn Harris
University of Charleston

Nancy Keffer, Chapter 1
Coordinator

Harriet Kopp
Berkeley County Schools

Sophia Peterson
West Virginia University

Doug Walters
Kanawha County Schools

Ann Wells
Princeton Senior High School

Vicki Wood, Kanawha County
Board of Education

Wisconsin:
Chairperson:
Tom Rondeau
Program Consultant

Committee:
Alfred L. Block
Educational Consultant

Phillip Ferguson
Waukesha Public Schools

Michael Hartoonian, Department
Public Instruction/Wisconsin

Jeanne M. Kress
Franklin Public Schools

Stephen Sansone
Waukesha South High School

Wyoming:
Chairperson:
Dick T. Kean Jr.
Program Consultant

Committee:
Karl Allen
Hot Springs County High School

Roger O. Hammer, Wyoming
Department of Education

Michael Horan
University of Wyoming

Renae Humburg, Laramie County
School District One

Gary L. McDowell, Laramie
County School District One

Donald Morris, Wyoming CSS

Sherry Tavegie
Wyoming Geographic Alliance

District of Columbia:
Chairperson:
Jack Hanna, Project Director, Phi
Alpha Delta Public Service Center
Committee:
Venetta Akwara, Woodrow Wilson
Senior High School

Mildred Musgrove
West Elementary School

Edna Pearson
Langdon Administrative Unit

ENGLISH AS A SECOND LANGUAGE REVIEW COMMITTEE

Deborah Short, Chair
Associate Division Director, ESL
Center for Applied Linguistics
Washington, District of Columbia

Denise McKeon, Director of
Outreach AERA, Washington,
District of Columbia

Joseph Bellino
Montgomery Blair High School
Silver Spring, Maryland

Jane Yedlin
Multifunctional Resource Center
Providence, Rhode Island

Maria Pacheco
Multifunctional Resource Center
Providence, Rhode Island

Myron Berkman, Newcomer High
School, Berkeley, California

OTHER REVIEWERS

Bill Abrams
Carson City, Nevada

Sister Mary Adelaine
Los Angeles, California

John Alexion
Providence, Rhode Island

Sharon Appleby
Lauredale, Pennsylvania

Eduardo J. Armijo
Seattle, Washington

April D. Ashley
Vancleave, Mississippi

Marc Bacon
Littleton, Colorado

Travis Ball, Jr.
Newport, Tennessee

Miller Barron
Marietta, Georgia

Dorris Boone
Austin, Texas

Sally Broughton
Bozeman, Montana

Marty Butt
Bakersfield, California

Jane Buxton
Spearfish, South Dakota

Elaine C. Chemistruck
Edgewood, New Mexico

Elaine Christensen
St. Clair Shores, Michigan

Josephine Cisneros
Fort Worth, Texas

Galen Clow
Erskine, Minnesota

Larry Cochran
Fort Smith, Arkansas

Paul Conway
Hasbrouck Heights, New Jersey

Gwen M. Cox
Lawton, Oklahoma

Jane Ann Craig
Austin, Texas

Dean Cristol
Greensboro, North Carolina

Janet W. Crouse
Chicago, Illinois

Paul Dain
Bloomfield Hills, Michigan

Anita Danker
Hopkinton, Massachusetts

Elizabeth H. Debra
Washington, District of Columbia

Patricia Dillman
Ocean Springs, Mississippi

Concetta Donvito
Parsippany, New Jersey

Robin E. Dorey
North Little Rock, Arkansas

Lori A. Doyle
Wichita, Kansas

John Drisko
Gorham, Maine

Maurice J. Duttera, Sr.
West Point, Georgia

Linda Eikenberry
Fort Worth, Texas

Bill Elkinton
Juneau, Alaska

Bill Ertmer
Meeker, Colorado

Sam Evans
Bowling Green, Kentucky

Muriel Evans
Providence, Rhode Island

Ronald P. Eydenberg
Revere, Massachusetts

Robert W. Fardy
Concord, Massachusetts

John Feldhusen
West Lafayette, Indiana

Jeff Ferguson
Des Moines, Iowa

Liz Fitzhugh
Malvern, Arkansas

Linda Foote
Cedarbug, Wisconsin

Jeff Friesen
Inman, Kansas

Julia M. Frohreich
Madison, Wisconsin

Robert Gabrick
Somerset, Wisconsin

Leo Gallegos
Houston, Texas

Joanne E. Galvan
San Antonio, Texas

Thomas Gamertsfelder
Neward, Ohio

Patricia Geyer
Sacramento, California

Elizabeth Gilman
Somersworth, New Hampshire

Marie Gosnell
Winchester, Massachusetts

Leroy Griswold
Haysville, Kansas

Millie Griswold
Wyandotte, Michigan

Bill Hagevig
Juneau, Arkansas

Julia P. Hardin
Winston-Salem, North Carolina

Marcey A. Harman
Laureldale, Pennsylvania

Kathy Hawks
Princeton, West Virginia

Rhonda Haynes
Austin, Texas

Pamela Henderson
Fort Worth, Texas

Ten Henson
Graham, North Carolina

Walt Herscher
Appleton, Wisconsin

Carol A. Hess
Spearfish, South Dakota

Elain Hicks
Greely, Colorado

James H. Hinshaw
Norfolk, Virginia

Victoria Hollister
Wheaton, Illinois

Robin S. Hom
San Leandro, California

Kathleen G. Hood
Spearfish, South Dakota

Megan Hoskins
Bellevue, Washington

Deneen Howard
Ripley, Oklahoma

Nina Hunt
Lawton, Oklahoma

Daniel T. Illiano
Cedar Grove, New Jersey

Marie Jamul
Medford, Massachusetts

Michael J. Jankanish
Tacoma, Washington

Don Joern
LaVista, Nebraska

Lonzena Jones
Silver Springs, Maryland

Laurel Martin Kanthak
Reston, Virginia

Marlene La Counte
Billings, Montana

Ann Lackey
Lake Oswego, Orgeon

Rolland Lassen
New Salem, North Dakota

Pam Locke
Vancleave, Mississippi

Teresa Maebori
Washington, DC

Lori Mammen
San Antonio, Texas

William Marmion
Long Beach, California

Mary Marockie
Wheeling, West Virginia

Esther L. Martens
Eden Prairie, Minnesota

John H. Mauldin
Pueblo West, Colorado

Nancy McCormick
Salt Lake City, Utah

Melinda McMahon
Hinsdale, Illinois

Shirley Mead-Mezzetta
Millbrae, California

Jack C. Morgan
Louisville, Kentucky

Michael Morris
Sitka, Alaska

William J. Muthig
Columbus, Ohio

Carol Newland
Spearfish, South Dakota

Pam Nortrip
Juneau, Alaska

Kim Noveloso
Ewa Beach, Hawaii

Mary Jane Nudell
East Grand Forks, Minnesota

Robert O'Connor
Cerritos, California

Linda Partridge
Foley, Minnesota

Collis D. Patterson
Baltimore, Maryland

James E. Pattison
Brookfield, Wisconsin

Nancy V. Paysinger
Atlanta, Georgia

Maureen Perkins
Hartford, Connecticut

Richard Peters
Corpus Christi, Texas

Barbara Peterson
Spearfish, South Dakota

Edward L. Phillips
Wyomissing, Pennsylvania

William J. Piacentini
Cranston, Rhode Island

Center for Civic Education

Peter Pitard
San Diego, California

Otis Porter
Falmouth, Massachusetts

Beverly Pruitt
Anchorage, Alaska

Charles H. Purdy
Naples, Florida

Linda Pursley
Vancleave, Mississippi

Ryan Lee Ransom
Edison, New Jersey

Orville Reddington
Boise, Idaho

Mary P. Reese
Arlington, Virginia

Carol S. Renner
Kearney, Nebraska

Katherine J. Revels
Raleigh, North Carolina

H. Riejo
Rochester, New York

Pamela L. Riley
Greensboro, North Carolina

Charlotte Risinger
Fort Worth, Texas

Sherry Roastingear
Durango, Colorado

Jeannie Robinson
Fort Worth, Texas

Douglas Rogers
Clayton, New York

Mark D. Rothman
Port Washington, New York

Robert R. Schneider
Spearfish, South Dakota

Steven W. Shockley
Gate City, Virginia

Alice Shoemake
Biloxi, Mississippi

Venetta Sloane-Akwara
Washington, DC

Nora Sperino
Pavilion, New York

J. Stanforth
Lehigh Acres, Florida

Joseph P. Stoltman
Kalamazoo, Michigan

Joan Thompson
Blackfoot, Idaho

Stephanie Thompson-Schecter
Niskayuna, New York

W. Scott Thomson
Greenville, North Carolina

Nicholas Topougis
Columbus, Ohio

Alexander Trento
Trenton, New Jersey

Anita Usacka
Notre Dame, Indiana

Ralph Vogel
Inman, Kansas

Catherine Waldo
Oklahoma City, Oklahoma

Paul Wieser
Glendale, Arizona

Ray Willmuth
Fort Worth, Texas

Gregory Wilsey
Albany, New York

Pat Wolff
Rapid City, South Dakota

Jean Wurst
University Heights, Ohio

Myron E. Yoder
Emmaus, Pennsylvania

Nancy Young
Forest, Virginia

PHOTO CREDITS

Cover photo courtesy of the National Park Service, Statue of Liberty National Monument.

Children's portraits by Eric Futran/Futran Photography.

Historic landmarks are with kind permission of Ralph D. Jones "The Splendor of Washington."

Center for Civic Education

A

B

C

Center for Civic Education

Center for Civic Education

CENTER FOR CIVIC EDUCATION

National Standards for Civics and Government

Now you can help schools achieve this nation's civic mission: to prepare informed, competent, and responsible citizens who possess a reasoned commitment to the values and principles essential to the preservation and improvement of American constitutional democracy. These standards specify what students should know and be able to do in the field of civics and government. Grades K-12. 187 pages. ISBN 0-89818-155-0.

Services and Curricular Materials

The Center for Civic Education has various services and materials available to assist individuals and institutions in implementing *National Standards for Civics and Government.*

Use this order form to receive additional information:

- ☐ Consulting services
- ☐ Presentations for professional meetings
- ☐ Editorial support services
- ☐ Leadership training
- ☐ Teacher training
- ☐ Curricular materials that promote the use of *National Standards for Civics and Government*

Name/Position _____

Institution _____

Address _____

City/State/Zip _____

Telephone ( )   Fax ( )

Send this form to the
Center for Civic Education
5146 Douglas Fir Road
Calabasas, CA 91302-1467
Toll Free (800) 350-4223
Fax (818) 591-9330

National Standards for Civics and Government		
1-9 Copies $14.00 each	10 or More Copies $12.50 each	Totals
Number Ordered at $14.00 each:	Number Ordered at $12.50 each:	
Make check or money order payable to **Center for Civic Education** 5146 Douglas Fir Road Calabasas, CA 91302-1467 Toll Free (800) 350-4223 • Fax (818) 591-9330	Subtotal	$
	California residents add appropriate sales tax	$
	Shipping and Handling add 10%	$
	TOTAL	$

Ship to:

Name _____

Position _____

Institution _____

Address _____

City/State/Zip _____

Telephone ( )

Bill to: (if different)   Purchase Order No. _____

Name _____

Signature _____

Institution _____

Address _____

City/State/Zip _____

Telephone ( )

CENTER FOR CIVIC EDUCATION

National Standards for Civics and Government
Now you can help schools achieve this nation's civic mission: to prepare informed, competent, and responsible citizens who possess a reasoned commitment to the values and principles essential to the preservation and improvement of American constitutional democracy. These standards specify what students should know and be able to do in the field of civics and government. Grades K-12. 187 pages. ISBN 0-89818-155-0.

✂ -

Services and Curricular Materials

The Center for Civic Education has various services and materials available to assist individuals and institutions in implementing *National Standards for Civics and Government.*

Use this order form to receive additional information:

☐ Consulting services
☐ Presentations for professional meetings
☐ Editorial support services
☐ Leadership training
☐ Teacher training
☐ Curricular materials that promote the use of *National Standards for Civics and Government*

Name/Position _____

Institution _____

Address _____

City/State/Zip _____

Telephone ( )   Fax ( ) _____

Send this form to the
Center for Civic Education
5146 Douglas Fir Road
Calabasas, CA 91302-1467
Toll Free (800) 350-4223
Fax (818) 591-9330

National Standards for Civics and Government		
1-9 Copies $14.00 each	10 or More Copies $12.50 each	Totals
Number Ordered at $14.00 each:	Number Ordered at $12.50 each:	
Make check or money order payable to **Center for Civic Education** 5146 Douglas Fir Road Calabasas, CA 91302-1467 Toll Free (800) 350-4223 • Fax (818) 591-9330	Subtotal	$
	California residents add appropriate sales tax	$
	Shipping and Handling add 10%	$
	TOTAL	$

Ship to:

Name _____

Position _____

Institution _____

Address _____

City/State/Zip _____

Telephone ( ) _____

Bill to: (if different)   **Purchase Order No.** _____

Name _____

Signature _____

Institution _____

Address _____

City/State/Zip _____

Telephone ( ) _____